Jan Hamer | Nadine Weiland

Urlaubsarchitektur
Volume 2

**Ferienhäuser und kleine Hotels
A Guide to Architectural Retreats**

ausgewählt von
selected by

**www.urlaubsarchitektur.de
www.holidayarchitecture.com**

Inhalt | Contents

Vorwort | Introduction

Seit 2007 besteht das Portal urlaubsarchitektur.de und veröffentlicht seitdem jede Woche ein neues, außergewöhnliches Urlausdomizil. Das vorliegende Buch Urlaubsarchitektur 2 stellt daraus 45 weitere Apartments, Ferienhäuser und kleine Hotels in ganz Europa vor, die durch ihre besondere Gestaltung ein außergewöhnliches Urlaubsambiente schaffen.

Den verschiedenen Häusern ist neben der besonderen Gestaltungsqualität gemeinsam, dass es meist sehr individuelle, mitunter ungewöhnliche Unterkünfte sind: Häufig sind die Häuser von den Betreibern selbst geplant oder gestaltet worden. Ein Besuch lässt Sie diese sehr persönliche Nähe spüren und bietet oft einen ganz neuen Zugang zu einer Urlaubsregion.

Viele der Häuser haben einen sehr starken regionalen Aspekt und berücksichtigen die lokalen Traditionen. Das Wechselspiel mit Landschaften oder urbaner Umgebung ergeben teilweise überraschende sowie reizvolle Kompositionen, in jedem Fall Ergeb-nisse, die auf die große Geste klassischer „Design-häuser" verzichten können.

Nach dem erfolgreichen Band Urlaubsarchitektur 1 zeigt das hier vorliegende zweite Buch die Besonderheit und den Facettenreichtum der „Urlaubsarchitektur", die zunehmend – auch durch die stark gewachsene Bekanntheit des Portals urlaubsarchitektur.de - als eigene Typologie verstanden wird.

The portal urlaubsarchitektur.de | holiday-architecture.com was created in 2007 and since then it has been publicising a new unusual holiday residence every week. This book presents a selection of 45 further apartments, holiday homes and small hotels throughout Europe, which provide an exceptional holiday atmosphere owing to their unique design.

What the various residences have in common, apart from their special design quality, is that they offer mostly very individual and unusual accommodation: in many cases the houses were planned or designed by the owners themselves. These personal touches are evident to the visitor and often open up a whole new perspective on a holiday region.

Many of the buildings have very prominent regional features. Some surprising and charming compositions are created by the interaction with landscapes or the urban surroundings, in any case these buildings have no need of the grand gestures of classical 'design houses'.

Following the successful first volume of holidayarchitecture, this second volume presents distinctive and multifaceted 'holiday architecture', which can increasingly be considered as having its own typology, also owing to the significantly increased awareness of the portal urlaubsarchitektur.de | holidayarchitecture.com.

La Maison d'Ulysse

Übersichtskarte | General Map

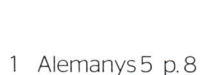

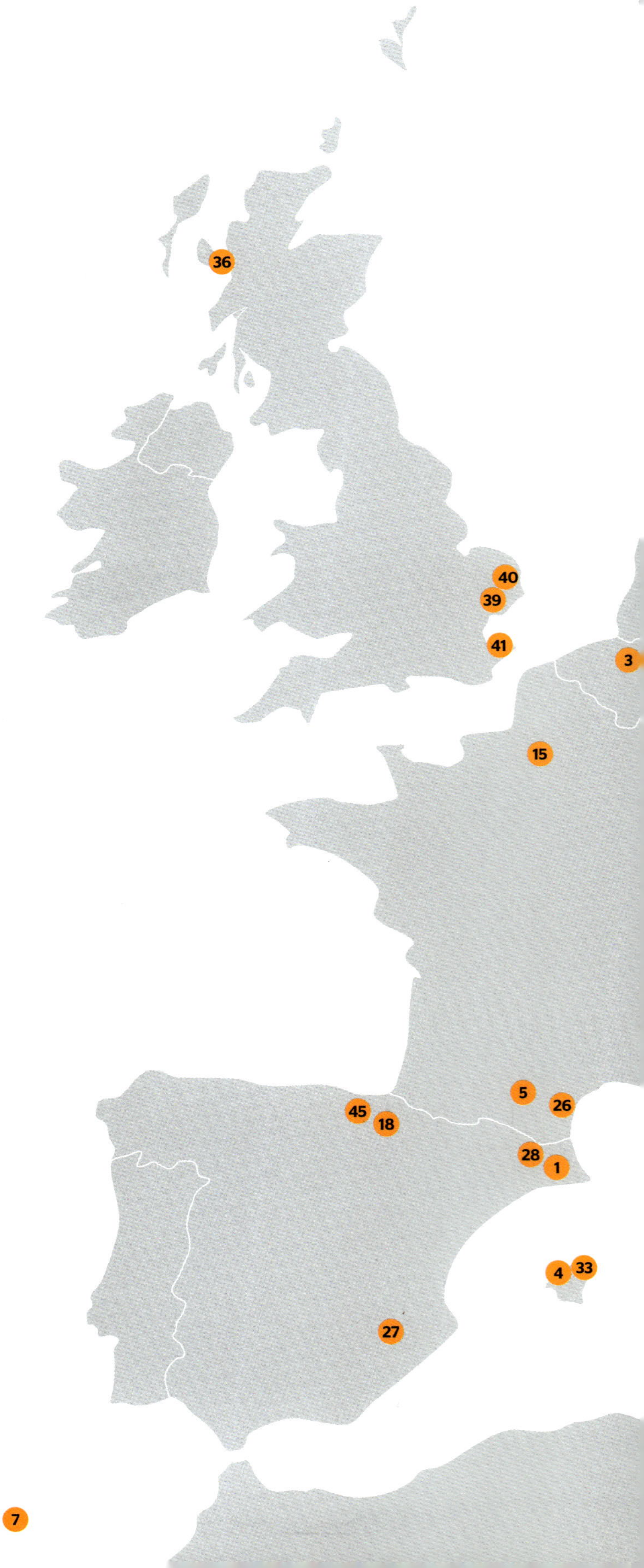

Alemanys 5

Spanien | Spain   Girona   Historische Altstadt | historical quarter

Carrer Alemany 5 , ES-17004 Girona
www.alemanys5.com, jmribera@gmail.com
Tel. +34 649 885136

Fertigstellung | date of completion: 2010 (Umbau | conversion)
Architekt | architect: Anna Noguera, ES-Barcelona
Architektur | architecture: alt & neu | old & new
Typ | accommodation: Apartments
Einheiten | units: 2 Zimmer | rooms

Alemanys 5 liegt in der charmanten katalanischen Stadt Girona. Von hier aus sind es nur 100 km bis in die Metropole Barcelona oder Perpignan in Frankreich. Die bekannte Costa Brava und damit der Strand ist in weniger als einer Stunde zu erreichen. Das Haus Alemanys 5 ist ein wundervoller Umbau eines Altbaus aus dem 16. Jahrhundert in einem der ältesten Viertel der Altstadt.
Die Architektin Anna Noguera aus Barcelona hat den Bestandsbau behutsam und elegant an- und umgebaut.
Die zahlreichen Ideen des Umbaus verblüffen und lassen einen zeitlosen Charakter entstehen. So sind Türen und Durchbrüche durch feine Stahlrahmen gekennzeichnet. Dieser Kontrast von zurückhaltender Moderne in der Kombination mit dem Altbau zeugt von großer Könnerschaft und erzeugt eine besondere Verbundenheit mit dem Bauwerk. Die alten Mauern kommen im Kontrast zu den modernen und dennoch warmen Materialien Holz, Beton und Stahl hervorragend zur Geltung.

Auf vier Geschossen verteilen sich die beiden schönen Apartments, die alle in erdigen Tönen ausgestattet wurden. Im vierten Obergeschoss bietet eine große Terrasse einen schönen Ausblick über die Stadt.
Das Apartment El Jardi (der Garten) ist 100 m² groß und umfasst neben den zwei Schlafzimmern, ein großes Badezimmer, ein großes Esszimmer mit einer Kitchenette und einem privaten Sonnengarten mit Swimming Pool im Erdgeschoss.
Die zweite Wohnung, El Badiu, verteilt 180 m² Wohnfläche über zwei Geschosse. Diese Wohnung bietet die große Sonnenterrasse mit Blick über die Altstadt. Eine großes Schlafzimmer und zwei Kinderzimmer, gut ausgestattete Küche, große, moderne Bäder sind Bestandteil. Sollte ein besonderer Service, beispielsweise ein Einkaufservice, gewünscht werden, kann dieser direkt gebucht werden.

Alemanys 5 lies in the charming Catalan town of Girona. It is only 100km from the metropolis of Barcelona or Perpignan in France. The famous Costa Brava and therefore the beach is less than an hour away.

The Alemanys 5 house is a wonderful conversion of an old 16th century building in one of the town's oldest districts. The architect Anna Noguera from Barcelona converted and extended the original building carefully and elegantly.

The array of conversion ideas is astounding, creating a timeless character. Doors and openings are characterised by steel frames. This contrast of reserved modernity set against the original building shows great expertise and creates a special affinity with the building. The old walls stand out strikingly against the modern but nevertheless warm materials of wood, concrete and steel.

The two apartments are divided across four floors, all furnished in earthy tones. On the 4th floor a large terrace provides a beautiful view over the town. The apartment El Jardi (The Garden) is 100m² and comprises two bedrooms, a large bathroom, a

spacious dining room with a kitchenette and a private sunny garden with a swimming pool at ground level. The second apartment, El Badiu, has a living space of 180m² split across two floors. This apartment offers a large sun terrace with views over the old town. It comprises a large bedroom with two children's rooms, an equipped kitchen and large modern bathrooms. If a special service is required, such as the shopping service, it can be booked directly.

art-lodge

Österreich | Austria   Verditz   Kärnten, Ostalpen | Carinthia, Eastern Alpes

Verditzerstr. 52, A-9542 Verditz/Afritz
www.art-lodge.com, info@art-lodge.at
Tel. +43 4247-2997 0, Fax +43 4247-29970 94

Fertigstellung | date of completion: 2008 (Umbau | conversion)
Architektur | architecture: alt & neu | old & new
Typ | accommodation: Hotel
Einheiten | units: 12 Zimmer/Suiten | 12 rooms/suites

Eingebettet in die malerische Landschaft der Kärntner Nockberge liegt die art-lodge am Verditz in 1.058 m Höhe. Hierhin zogen die früheren Werbeprofis Katrin und Dirk Liesenfeld von Düsseldorf, um sich ihren Traum vom einzigartigen Kunsthotel mit Avantgarde-Kunst und einer Galerie zu erfüllen.

Der 300 Jahre alte Rohrerhof wurde ihr neues Zuhause. Nach dem behutsamen Umbau in den Jahren 2007/2008 präsentiert sich der alte Hof in einer Mischung aus Tradition und Kunstmoderne. Hier geht alte kärntner Baukunst eine interessante Symbiose mit moderner Kunst und schickem Design ein. Visuell wurde hier nicht gespart und so kann an jeder Ecke ein weiteres Detail entdeckt werden. Die Macher nennen das Konzept „sehr lebendig". Die alte Scheune wurde ebenfalls in das Hotel mit einbezogen. Diese wurde saniert und sensibel zu einem hellen und komfortablen Gästehaus ausgebaut. Es umfasst zusätzlich einen 100 m² großen Galeriesaal, der für Ausstellungen, Meetings oder Veranstaltungen genutzt werden kann. Insgesamt 12 unterschiedlich große Zimmer und Suiten können gemietet werden. Die Versorgung mit Wärme wurde weitestgehend unter strengen ökologischen Maßstäben hergerichtet. So wird das neue Solarsystem durch eine Pelletsheizung unterstützt, die mit Holzresten aus dem nahen Feistritz befeuert wird.

Im gesamten Haus stehen Werke von Künstlern, die weitestgehend aus Düsseldorf kommen. In der letzten Zeit sind auch Artefakte anderer Orte und Nationen dazugekommen. Neben der hochwertigen Ausstattung eines Viersternehotels gehen die Kunstwerke so einen gänzlich neuen Kontext ein.

Das angeschlossene Restaurant mit nur 24 Sitzen erprobt lokale Nahrungsmittel, wie Biofleisch, in einer Zubereitung, die die Besitzer aus der gesamten Welt zusammen sammeln.
In diesem Zusammenhang wird Kunst nochmals in einen neuen Rahmen gestellt. Durch sogenannte „high-art cooking" oder „music and dinner" Events wird zur lebhaften Auseinandersetzung mit der zeitgenössischen Kunst angeregt.
Im Sommer als Hotel betrieben, kann die art-lodge auch ganzjährig als großes Ferienhaus gemietet werden – entweder nur das Haupthaus mit 6 Zimmern für 12 Erwachsene und 5 Kinder oder Haupthaus und Scheune für insgesamt 24 Erwachsene und 7 Kinder. Ob als Selbstversorger oder mit dem kompletten "art-lodge package" - die absolute Privatsphäre sorgt immer für besonderen Luxus.

Nestled into the picturesque landscape of the Carinthian Nockberge lies the art-lodge on Verditz mountain at 1058m above sea level. The former advertising professionals Katrin and Dirk Liesenfeld from Düsseldorf moved here to fulfil their dream of a unique art hotel with avant-garde art and a gallery.

The 300-year-old Rohrerhof became their new home. After a careful conversion in 2007/2008 the old house presents itself as a combination of tradition and modern art. It is an interesting symbiosis of old Carinthian architecture; modern art and elegant design. It is visually rich and in every corner one can discover a further detail. The creators call this concept 'very vital'. The old barn was also incorporated into the hotel. It was renovated and thoughtfully converted into a light and comfortable guest house. The hotel also comprises a 100m² gallery hall, which can be used for exhibitions, meetings or events. A total of 12 rooms and suites of different sizes can be rented.

The heating system largely conforms to strict ecological standards. The new solar panels are supported by pellet heating, using wood scraps from nearby Feistritz.

Throughout the house are works by artists mostly from Düsseldorf. Recently artefacts from other places and nations have been added too. Alongside the high-quality furnishing of a four star hotel the works of art are displayed in a whole new context.

The adjoining restaurant with just 24 seats offers local produce, such as organic meat, as part of recipes that the owners have collected around the world.
This provides a further setting for the theme of art.
Through so-called 'high-art cooking' or 'music and dinner' events one is encouraged to engage actively with contemporary art.
Used as a hotel in summer, the art-lodge can be rented the whole year round as a large holiday home-either just the main house with 6 rooms for 12 adults and 5 children, or the main house and barn for a total of 24 adults and 7 children. Whether self-catering or with the complete 'art-lodge package', the absolute privacy always provides a special luxury.

B&B Sofie Lachaert

Belgien | Belgium   Tielrode   Flandern | Flanders

St. Jozefstraat 30, BE-9140 Tielrode
www.sofielachaert.be, info@lachaert.com
Tel. + 32 37111963

Fertigstellung | date of completion: 2008
Architekt | architect: Luc d'Hanis & Sofie Lachaert, BE-Tielrode
Architektur | architecture: alt & neu | old & new
Typ | accomodation: Hotel / B&B
Einheiten | units: 12 Zimmer | rooms

In der kleinen Stadt Tielrode in Belgien, die in der schönen Auenlandschaft des Zusammenflusses der Durme und der Schelde liegt, haben im Jahr 2000 Sofie Lachaert und Luc d'Hanis eine Bed&Breakfast Unterkunft eröffnet. Von hier aus sind es nur 15 Minuten mit dem Auto nach Antwerpen und 30 Minuten nach Gent oder Brüssel.

Am Ende einer kleinen Straße, die zur Fähre am Fluss führt, liegen die Galerie und die Ateliers der beiden Künstler, die in einen Altbau eingefügt wurden. Die Innenausstattung wurde ebenfalls von den Eigentümern vorgenommen. Sie haben sich für eine Verbindung von Altem und Neuem entschieden. So konnte das Künstleroeuvre in die Gestaltung mit einfliessen. Viele der Einrichtungsgegenstände sind Kunstwerke, die bei Gefallen erworben werden können. So ändert sich die Inneneinrichtung permanent und lässt die Einrichtung lebendig werden.

Die Sanierung und der Umbau der Bestandsbauten bedeutete, dass die gesamten Innenräume bis hin zu den Wandkonstruktionen freigelegt werden mussten. Dieses Konzept aber entsprach den Ideen der beiden Künstler. Neue, abgehängte Decken reichen nur teilweise über die neu, in abgedunkeltem weiss gestrichenen Decken, um die alte Höhe und die originale Konstruktion sichtbar zu machen.

Die Inneneinrichtung ist schlicht und mit modernen Gegenständen und Möbeln ausgestattet. Aber auch hier wurde auf die Verbindung von traditionellen Gestaltungen mit modernen Acht gelegt. Alte Stühle treffen hier auf alte Tische, modernes Besteck, von Künstlern entworfen, treffen auf altes Geschirr.

In the small Belgian town of Tielrode, which lies in the beautiful pasture landscape at the confluence of the Durme and the Schelde, Sofie Lachaert and Luc d'Hanis opened a bed & breakfast in 2000. It is just 15 minutes by car to Antwerpen and 30 minutes to Gent or Brussels.

At the end of a small road leading to the river ferry lie the gallery and ateliers of the two artists, which were incorporated into a old building. The interior design was also undertaken by the owners. They decided on a combination of old and new, and so their artistic works were able to flow into the design. Many of the interior items are works of art which can be purchased on request, and so the dynamic and lively interior is constantly changing.

The renovation and conversion of the existing buildings required the exposure of all the interior rooms down to the wall construction, but this concept suited the ideas of the two artists. New suspended ceilings only partly cover the new ceilings painted in darkened white, so as to make the former height and original construction visible.
The interior design is elegantly simple and equipped with modern objects and furniture, emphasising further the blending of tradition and modern design elements. Old chairs are combined with old tables, and modern cutlery designed by artists alongside old crockery.

Das perfekte Ferienhaus

Das perfekte Ferienhaus verbindet zwei der beliebtesten Vergnügungen des Menschen: Architektur und Reisen. Indem wir versuchen zu entdecken, welche Vorstellungen wir von unserem idealen Ferienhaus haben, erfüllen wir auch die wichtige Aufgabe, besser zu verstehen, welche Mängel unsere gewöhnliche Wohnumgebung aufweist. Wir müssen aus dem einfachen Grund verreisen, dass Häuser auf unsere Gefühle - und dadurch auf das, was wir sein könnten - einen großen Einfluss ausüben. Die Häuser, in denen wir normalerweise leben, so angenehm sie auch sein mögen, werden immer durch ihre Stabilität und Vertrautheit beeinträchtigt. An schlechten Tagen lösen sie eine Art Klaustrophobie aus, für die es keine Heilung gibt, außer sich von einer Reiseagentur die stark übelteuerte, aber unwiderstehlich elegante Betonvilla im Tessin oder die verlockend schmucklose Hütte aus schwarzem Schindel in Island schmackhaft machen zu lassen.

Es gibt Zeiten, in denen wir uns mit neuen Einrichtungen und Aussichten umgeben müssen, um innere Übergänge zum Ausdruck zu bringen. Unsere Sinne sterben ab, wenn wir zu viel Zeit zuhause verbringen. Wir hören auf, Räume, Gerüche und Licht wahrzunehmen. Aber wenn wir in einem Ferienhaus ankommen, sind wir plötzlich so feinsinnig, als ob wir aus unserer eigenen Haut geschlüpft sind. Wir erinnern uns an die vielfältigen Möglichkeiten, die Küche zu gestalten. Wir fragen uns, wie es wäre, ein Geschirrset in zitronengelb zu haben. Wir werden uns darüber bewusst, wie wichtig morgens die Ausrichtung des Hauses ist und welchen Unterschied es machen kann, wenn jemand sich die Zeit genommen hat, sorgfältig über die Positionierung eines Stillleben mit Erdbeere oder über die Rolle eines Gemüsegartens nachzudenken.
Ferienhäuser bedeuten dasselbe für Architektur wie

Affären für Ehen: Sie können sich den Luxus erlauben, unpraktisch, romantisch und irrsinnig nachgiebig zu sein. Wir können für zwei Wochen etwas genießen, was auf die Dauer unerträglich wäre. Bei der Auswahl eines Ferienhauses ist es möglich, untergeordneten Aspekten unserer Persönlichkeit freien Raum zu geben, die wir in unserem alltäglichen Wohnhaus aufopfern mussten. Wir können dem Teil von uns freien Lauf lassen, dem verzierte italienische Möbel aus dem neunzehnten Jahrhundert oder der Geruch von bayerischer Kiefernholzverkleidung heimlich gefallen.
Wir können vortäuschen, Besitzer eines Pfarrhauses, einer Zenwohnung, eines Lofts in Zürich oder eines Bootshauses in Sydney zu sein. Die Ferienhäuser, die wir mieten, sind von vielen lästigen praktischen Anforderungen an unsere gewöhnlichen Wohnräume befreit. Sie können es sich erlauben, eine unverantwortliche Platzaufteilung zu haben, uns lediglich einen einzigen schmalen Schrank zur Verfügung zu stellen, aber dafür Raum für unnötigen Luxus wie riesige offene Kamine oder überraschend positionierte Fenster und Galerien zu bieten. Und so charmant Hotels auch sein mögen, es ist - wie Kinder wissen - ein besonderes Vergnügen, für eine Weile Hausbesitzer zu spielen. Nur dann, wenn wir in einem fremden Land den Kühlschrank aufgefüllt haben, fangen wir an, den Ort zu verstehen.

Aber der Reiz von Ferienhäusern ist nicht auf die Zeit beschränkt, in der wir sie bewohnen. So wie alle Reiseerlebnisse helfen sie uns, nach Hause zurückzukehren mit einem größeren Bewusstsein von den Vorteilen unseres eigenen Wohnraums und mit einer neuen Verbundenheit gegenüber unseren Dingen und der Auswahl, die wir getroffen haben.

Alain de Botton wurde 1969 in der Schweiz geboren und studierte in Cambridge Geschichte und Philosophie. Heute lebt er als Schriftsteller, Journalist und TV-Produzent mit seiner Familie in London. Seine Bücher befassen sich mit philosophischen Ideen für die Probleme der Gegenwart und gesellschaftspolitischen Fragen.
Seine bekanntesten Werke sind *Die Kunst des Reisens* sowie *Glück und Architektur: Von der Kunst, daheim zu Hause zu sein*.

Alain de Botton hegt schon lange eine Leidenschaft für moderne Architektur. Er verfasste nicht nur ein Buch zu diesem Thema, sondern spielte auch eine entscheidende Rolle bei der Gründung von *Living Architecture* - einer Organisation, die etablierte Weltklassearchitekten und herausragende Nachwuchstalente damit beauftragt, an verschiedenen Orten in Großbritannien Häuser zu bauen. Diese Häuser stehen der Öffentlichkeit als Ferienwohnungen zur Miete zur Verfügung. Damit möchte *Living Architecture* der Allgemeinheit die Erfahrung ermöglichen, in Räumen zu leben, zu essen und zu schlafen, die von einem herausragenden Architekturbüro gestaltet wurden.

The perfect holiday house

The perfect holiday house promises a simultaneous taste of two of humans' favourite pleasures: architecture and travel. And in seeking to discover what our ideal holiday house could be, we are also undertaking the important task of understanding a little better what is wrong with where we normally live.

We need to get away for the simple reason that houses exert a powerful influence on what we feel and in turn, on who we can be. The houses we usually live in, however delightful they are, will always be undermined by their stability and familiarity. On a bad day, they induce a kind of claustrophia for which there is no effective cure other than to consult a travel agent about the ruinously-priced but irresistibly elegant concrete villa in the Ticino or the enticingly austere black shingle cabin in Iceland.

There are times when we need to surround ourselves with new furnishings and views to help cement inner transitions. Our senses go dead if we spend too long at home, we cease to notice rooms, smells and lights. But transported to a holiday house, we are suddenly as sensitive as if we had slipped out of our own skins. We remember the range of possibilities of organising a kitchen. We marvel at what it would be like to have an entirely lemon-yellow crockery set. We realise the profound importance of where a house faces in the morning and what a difference it can make when someone has taken care to think carefully about the positioning of a still-life of a strawberry or the role of a vegetable garden.

Holiday houses are to architecture what affairs are to marriages: they can afford the luxury of being impractical, romantic and absurdly indulgent. We can enjoy for two weeks what would be unbearable if it were forever. In choosing a house, we are allowed to give room to subsidiary sides of our characters that we have had to sacrifice in our day-to-day residence. We can give free reign to the part of us that covertly rather enjoys ornate 19th century Italian furniture or the smell of Bavarian pine pannelling. We can play at being the owner of a vicarage or a Zen apartment, a Zurich loft or a Sydney boat-house. The houses we rent can be freed of many tedious practical requirements of regular lodgings. They can afford to be irresponsible with space, allowing us only a single narrow cupboard, and yet to make way for indulgences like gigantic fireplaces or implausibly positioned windows and galleries. And whatever the charms of hotels, there are – as children know – particular pleasures in playing house for a time. It isn't really until we have stocked up a fridge in a foreign country that we have begun to understand the place.

But the attraction of holiday houses isn't limited to the period when we are living in them. Like all experiences of travel, they help us to return home more aware of the advantages of our own spaces and with a renewed commitment to the objects and choices we have made.

Alain de Botton was born in Switzerland in 1969 and studied history and philosophy in Cambridge. Now he lives in London with his family and works as an author, journalist and TV presenter. His books are concerned with philosophical ideas in relation to contemporary problems and with socio-political issues.
The most well-known are: *The Art of Travel* and *The Architecture of Happiness*.

Alain has long been passionate about modern architecture. Aside from writing a book on the subject, Alain was instrumental in starting a new organisation called *Living Architecture*, which has asked a series of established and emerging world-class architects to build houses around the UK. The houses are available to rent for holidays by the general public. The inspiration for *Living Architecture* came from a desire for people to be able to experience what it is like to live, eat and sleep in a space designed by an outstanding architectural practice.

Casa al Mar

Spanien | Spain   Port Sóller   Mallorca

Calle de Buñyola 39 , ES-07100 Port Sóller
www.casa-al-mar.com, info@casa-al-mar.com
Tel. +34 971 632 560

Fertigstellung | date of completion: 2007
Architekt | architect: Anke Scheideler, ES-Port Sóller
Architektur | architecture: modern
Typ | accommodation: Ferienhaus | holiday house
Einheiten | units: 1 Haus | 1 house

Das CASA AL MAR liegt im Hafen von Port Sóller. Seine Ausrichtung zum offenen Meer mit Blick über den ganzen Hafen und dem beeindruckenden Tramuntana-Gebirge im Hintergrund gehört zu den begehrtesten der ganzen Insel. In ca. 800 m erreicht man die Promenade und den Strand von Port Sóller mit seinem romantischen Ambiente.

Mit viel Liebe zum Detail haben die Eigentümer dieses Haus geplant und auch errichtet. Aufgrund der jahrelangen Architektur- und Bauerfahrung auf der Insel war es den Eigentümern wichtig, moderne, klare Architektur mit den traditionellen Materialien und der Formsprache südlicher Bauweise zu vereinen. Zusätzlich wurde großer Wert auf energetische Nachhaltigkeit bei der Ausführung gelegt. Die Wärmedämmwerte entsprechen einem Niedrigenergiehaus, das Warmwasser (auch für die Fußbodenheizung) wird mittels einer Luftwärmepumpe erzeugt. Eine dicke Außenhülle und doppelte Dachisolierung schützt vor der Sommerhitze und hält die Wärme im Winter. Das Haus zeichnet sich durch seinen modern-mediterranen Baustil aus. Typische Bauelemente, wie bodentiefe Fenster, zweiflügelige Innentüren, Zementmosaikplatten als Bodenbelag, Holzklappläden und Natursteinmauern im Außenbereich wurden aufgegriffen und zeitgemäß interpretiert. Auch ein Teil des Mobiliars wurde für dieses Haus von den Eigentümern entworfen und speziell angefertigt.

Das CASA AL MAR verfügt über 200 qm Wohnfläche auf zwei Etagen, drei Schlafräume, drei Bäder (davon eins en suite), einen großzügigen Wohn- und Essbereich mit Panoramablick auf den Hafen und das Meer, eine offene Küche mit Kochinsel und einen Kamin im Wohnbereich. Alle Schlafräume und Arbeitszimmer haben separate Klimaanlagen.
Der Außenbereich mit Terrasse befindet sich auf der Wohnebene mit Außenküche. Eine weitere Dachterrasse mit Pool und Holzdeck liegt oberhalb des Hauses. Von allen Terrassen kann ein unübertroffener Blick über den Hafen und das offene Meer mit den fantastischen Sonnenuntergängen der Westküste genossen werden.

The CASA AL MAR lies in the harbour of Port Sóller. Its location facing the open sea with a view over the whole harbour and the impressive Tramuntana mountains in the background is amongst the most sought-after of the whole island.

The promenade and the beach of Port Sóller with its romantic atmosphere is about 800m away.
The owners planned and built the house with keen attention to detail. Because of their years of architecture and building experience on the island, it was important for the owners to blend modern clear-cut architecture with the traditional materials and forms of the southern building style. Furthermore a lot of emphasis was placed on implementing energy sustainability.
The house is characterised by its modern Mediterranean building style. Traditional building elements were used and interpreted in a contemporary style, such as full-length windows, interior double doors, cement mosaic panels as the flooring material, wooden shutters and natural stone walls on the exterior. Part of the furniture for the house was also designed and especially made by the owners.

The CASA AL MAR comprises a living space of 200m² on two floors, three bedrooms, three bathrooms (of which one is en suite), a generous living and dining area with panoramic views over the harbour and the sea, an open-plan kitchen with a cooking island and a fireplace in the living room. All bedrooms and studies have separate air conditioning. The outside space with a terrace and an open-air kitchen is on the same floor as the living room. A further roof terrace with a pool and wooden decking lies above the house. From all terraces one can enjoy an unrivalled view over the harbour and the open sea with the west coast's fantastic sunsets.

CasaCailla

Frankreich | France   Cailla   Mediterrane Pyrenäen | Eastern Pyrenees

![bedroom interior]

8, Rue des Lavoirs, FR-11140 Cailla
www.casacailla.com, info@casacailla.com

Fertigstellung | date of completion: 2011
Architekt | architect: S. Oelker und M. Glück, FR-Cailla
Architektur | architecture: alt & neu | old & new
Typ | accomodation: Ferienhaus | holiday house
Einheiten | units: 2 Häuser | 2 houses

Das CASA CAILLA liegt 500 m über dem Meeresspiegel, zwischen den Hochgebirgszügen der mediterranen Pyrenäen und der Mittelmeerküste.
In unmittelbarer Umgebung liegen die Burgen der Katharer ebenso wie die weiten Weinfelder des größten Weinanbaugebietes Frankreichs, inmitten der weichen Hügellandschaft der Vorgebirge mit ihren alten Wanderwegen. Die Strände des Mittelmeeres, die historischen Altstädte von Carcassonne und Perpignan sowie die Skigebiete und traumhaften Gebirgsseen des Hochgebirges sind innerhalb einer Fahrtstunde erreichbar.

Das CASA CAILLA ist ein exklusives Ferienhaus von hoher architektonischer Qualität in einer traumhaften Umgebung. Das alte Steinhaus mit seinen Scheunen liegt in einem friedlichen, mittelalterlichen Dorf mit nur 25 Einwohnern. Das Architektenpaar Simone Oelker und Michael Glück hat das alte Gebäude liebevoll restauriert. Das Gehöft besteht aus zwei unabhängigen Häusern: dem ehemaligen Haupthaus Casa 6 und der Scheune Casa 8, die ein offener Hof miteinander verbindet. Die ersten Bauten stammen aus dem 17. Jahrhundert und wurden aus Bruchstein der Umgebung erbaut.

Casa 6 (Fertigstellung 2012): Eine großzügige Dachverglasung sowie hohe Fensterelemente nach Süden zum Hof erzeugen eine feierliche, fast sakrale Anmutung. Zwei Schlafräume mit dazugehörigen Bädern werden über den vertikalen Luftraum erschlossen, welcher ebenerdig einen großzügigen Küchen- und Essbereich bietet und im zweites Geschoss mit einer Loungeebene zwischen der vertikalen Offenheit des

Innenraums und den abgeschlossenen Schlafbereichen vermittelt. Eine geschützte Dachterrasse schließt die vertikale Raumfolge ab und bietet einen traumhaften Ausblick über das Rébentytal.

Casa 8: Durch die Offenheit und Größe des ebenerdigen Küchen- und Essbereichs konnten die Anmutung der Steinscheune erhalten bleiben, Durchblicke und Durchlässe zu der darüber liegenden Loungeebene geschaffen und die beiden Schlafebenen voneinander getrennt werden. Damit bildet die Steinscheune das kommunikative Zentrum des Hauses und ist gleichzeitig verbindendes und trennendes Element. Die beiden Schlafebenen sind abgeschlossene, autarke Einheiten.

CASA CAILLA lies at 500m above sea level, between the high mountain ranges of the Mediterranean Pyrenees and the Mediterranean coast. In the immediate surroundings lie the Cathar Castles as well as the extensive vineyards of the largest wine-growing region in France, amidst the gently rolling foothills with their old hiking paths.

The Mediterranean beaches, the historical old towns of Carcassonne and Perpignan, the ski resorts and delightful high mountain lakes are within an hour's drive.

CASA CAILLA is an exclusive holiday residence of high architectural quality in magical surroundings. The old stone house with its barns lies in a peaceful medieval village with just 25 inhabitants. The architectural couple Simone Oelker and Michael Glück renovated the old building lovingly. The homestead consists of two independent houses: the former main house Casa 6 and the barn Casa 8, joined via an open courtyard. The oldest buildings originated in the 17th century and were built with local quarry-stone.

Casa 6 (completion 2012): Generous roof glazing and high window elements towards the south facing the courtyard create a ceremonious, almost sacral impression. Two bedrooms with their respective bathrooms are accessed via a vertical open space, which offers a spacious kitchen and dining area at ground level. On the second floor a lounge area connects the vertical openness of the interior space to the closed bedrooms. A sheltered roof terrace rounds off the vertical arrangement of the rooms and affords magnificent views over the Rèbenty valley.

Casa 8: owing to the openness and size of the ground floor kitchen and dining area it was possible to maintain the appearance of stone barns, to create open views and openings towards the lounge level above and to divide the two bedrooms from each other. The stone barn is therefore the communication centre of the house and it acts as a connecting and dividing element at the same time. The two sleeping floors are joined autonomous units.

Die Halde

Deutschland | Germany   Oberried-Hofsgrund   Schwarzwald | Black Forrest

D-79254 Oberried-Hofsgrund
www.halde.com, info@halde.com
Tel. +49 7602 94470

Fertigstellung | date of completion: 2000
Architekt | architect: Werkgruppe Lahr, D-Lahr/Schwarzwald
Architektur | architecture: alt & neu | old & new
Typ | accommodation: Hotel
Einheiten | units: 38 Zimmer | rooms

Im Schwarzwald. Aufstieg zum Schauinsland auf
1.147 Meter Höhe. Die Halde. Ein Urgestein. Sie besteht
schon mehr als 850 Jahre. Die erstmalige Erwähnung
als "Dyselmuthof" findet sich bereits im Jahre 1142.
Die Geschichte der „neuen Halde" erfährt von 1997
bis ins Jahr 2000 eine zukunftsweisende Zäsur:
Das Bauerngehöft wird unter Leitung des Architekten
Carl Langenbach von der Werkgruppe Lahr behutsam saniert. Die Architektur folgt der eindrücklichen
Vorgabe der Natur: Aus der Distanz ist das Haus ein
fast verschwindender Punkt, eingebettet in die
Landschaft des Schwarzwaldes. Aus der Nähe ist es
ein Ausrufezeichen. In Form, Farbe und Materialien
zeigt das Gebäude zugleich Respekt und
Selbstbewusstsein. Die traditionelle Holzschindel ist
prägnantes Kleid für das Walmdach und die Fassade.
Das Ensemble aus Altbau und Neubau bedient sich
mit dem Baustoff Holz eines jahrhundertelang
bewährten Materialkonzepts. Reduziert und schlicht,
aber warm und erdig
im Ausdruck.

2007 führt Carl Langenbach diese besondere Ästhe-
tik in einem Erweiterungsbau fort: Das Schauinsland
Badehaus fügt sich mit 2 Etagen zu Füßen des Haupt-
hauses ein - mit einzigartigem Blick zum Feldberg.
Die Würdigung für das gesamte Areal der Halde zeigt
sich jüngst in der Verleihung des Architekturpreises
2010 zur Baukultur Schwarzwald.
Wenn also seit 10 Jahren die Halde unter der Führung
von Lucia und Martin Hegar „1.147 m Hochgenuss"
verspricht, bedeutet dies für die Architektur wie auch
für alle anderen Bereiche: Vielfalt und Einfachheit zugleich. Qualität ohne Schnörkel.
In den Zimmern: In der Zurückhaltung entfalten Einrichtung und Stoffe ihre Aussagekraft. In der Halde-
Küche: Ursprüngliche, bodenständige Gerichte, lebendig und kreativ interpretiert. Es geht um Produkte,
nicht um Effekte. Hausherr Martin Hegar und seine
Mannschaft kochen vorwiegend mit heimischen
Zutaten von kleinen Käsereien, umliegenden Höfen
und regionalen Metzgereien. Genießen kann der Gast
in gemütlichen Schwarzwald-Stuben oder in hellen,
lichten Räumen mit Blick ins Panorama. Was im
Äußeren als Symbiose beginnt, setzt sich im Inneren
des Hauses nahtlos fort: Alt und neu verbinden sich.

Die Angebote im Schauinsland Badehaus wie auch
draußen in der Natur reichen von purer Entspannung
bis zum sportlichen Aktiv sein. Immer ganzheitlich
abgestimmt auf die natürlichen Bedürfnisse des Körpers und der Seele. Immer fachlich fundiert und begleitet: Ob Massagen, Tai Chi, Nordic Walking oder
Schneeschuhwanderung.

In the Black Forest one ascends to Schauinsland at an altitude of 1.147 metres, where 'Die Halde' ('The Pithead') and its primary rock have existed for more than 850 years. It was first mentioned as the 'Dyselmuthof' as early as 1142 a.c. The history of the 'Neue Halde' ('New Pithead') underwent a pioneering transformation from 1997 to 2000: the farmstead was renovated carefully under the direction of the architect Carl Langenbach from the Lahr work group. The architecture traces the impressive contours of the natural landscape: from a distance the house tapers away and almost disappears into the Black Forest landscape into which it is embedded. From close up the building resembles an exclamation mark, displaying respect for the surroundings as well as confidence in its form, colour and materials. The hipped roof and the façade are strikingly cladded with traditional wooden shingle. The use of wood as a material in the ensemble of old and new builds follows a centuries-old and time-proven concept - minimalistic and elegant but creating a warm and earthy atmosphere.

In 2007 Carl Langenbach carried this particular aesthetic over into the building of an extension: the two storeys of the Schauinsland Bathhouse

were added onto the base of the main house, with exceptional views towards Feldberg. The whole 'Die Halde' site recently received the Architectural Award 2010 with regard to Black Forest building culture, proving how it is appreciated and valued. Under the management of Lucia and Martin Hegar 'Die Halde' has been offering 'delectation at 1142 m for the last 10 years, meaning both richness and simplicity, high quality without any superfluous flourishes, in terms of the architecture and all other aspects. The rooms feature modest furnishings and textiles.

The Halde kitchen offers original local dishes, interpreted in an innovative and creative way. It is about the produce, not about creating effects. The owner Martin Hegar and his team cook mostly with regional ingredients from small cheese dairies, surrounding farms and local butchers. Guests can enjoy their meals in cosy Black Forest parlours or in light open rooms with panoramic views. What starts as a symbiosis on the exterior is carried over seam-lessly into the interior, with new and old merging.

The leisure options offered by the Schauinsland Bathhouse and outdoors in the surrounding nature range from pure relaxation to sporting activity, always holistically attuned to the natural needs of body and spirit and always accompanied by skilled knowledge and guidance, whether massages, Tai Chi, Nordic walking or hiking with snow shoes.

Estalagem da Ponta do Sol

Portugal   Ponta do Sol   Madeira

Caminho do Passo 6 , PT-Madeira 9360-529 Ponta do Sol
www.pontadosol.com, info@pontadosol.com
Tel. +351 291 970200, Fax +351 291 970209

Fertigstellung | date of completion: 2001
Architekt | architect: Tiago Oliveira, PT-Madeira
Architektur | architecture: modern
Typ | accommodation: Hotel
Einheiten | units: 54 Zimmer | rooms

In 25 km Entfernung von der Hauptstadt der portugiesischen Insel Madeira befindet sich seit 2001 auf einem steil abfallenden Felsen das magische Hotel Estalagem da Ponta do Sol.

In eine enge Schlucht unterhalb des Hotels drängt sich der kleine Ort Ponta do Sol an der Südküste Madeiras. Das ursprünglich gebliebene Dorf bietet reizvolle Ausblicke auf den Ozean. Der Name Ponta do Sol beinhaltet auch die vielen Sonnenstunden an denen sich der Ort erfreuen kann. Hinter der Palmenpromenade des Ortes liegt ein kleiner Kieselstrand.

Auf der gegenüberliegenden Seite drängen sich die weißen Häuser mit ihren roten Dächern zwischen zerklüfteten Hängen mit flachen Terrassierungen. Hoch auf den Felsen über dem Atlantik ist die Lage spektakulär. Das dort gelegene Hotel entstand aus der Renovierung einer alten "Quinta". Als Architekt zeichnet Tiago Oliveira verantwortlich. Das Anwesen wurde also als Weingut genutzt. Das Ziel war einen eigenständigen, zeitgemäßen Stil mit den Originalgebäuden und der besonderen Örtlichkeit zu verbinden. Die Architektur betont die Schönheit dieses speziellen Ortes und die entspannte Atmosphäre.

Auf mehrere Baukörper verteilt umfasst das Haus 54 Zimmer von denen alle einen Balkon besitzen. Ein Restaurant mit abenteuerlich-gewagter Lage direkt am Abhang bietet hervorragende Küche. Eine Pool- sowie eine Nachtbar nebst obligatorischer Aussichtsterrasse entspricht den Idealvorstellungen eines Cocktails am Meer.

Sollte das Wetter mal nicht kataloghaft perfekt sein, bietet ein Spa mit Dampfsaunen, Jacuzzis und allen weiteren notwenigen Ausstattungsdetails perfekte Abwechslung.

Die Architektur reagiert auf die Hanglage und passt sich dieser durch grosse Tarrassierungen und natürlichen Materialien an. Durch die Aufteilung der Räume in mehrere Bauten ist eine Anlage entstanden, die große Maßstäbe vermeidet. Besonders witzig: Eine Stahlbrücke, die so etwas wie eine kleine Stadt andeutet, verbindet Bauten über den Hang hinweg. Die Inneneinrichtung ist zurückhaltend modern, ohne Design in den Vordergrund stellen zu wollen.

The magical Hotel Estalagem da Ponta do Sol opened in 2001 and is located on a steep cliff 25km from the capital of the Portuguese island of Madeira. The small village of Ponta do Sol on Madeira's south coast is huddled in a narrow gorge below the hotel. The village has remained unchanged and affords delightful ocean views. The name Ponta do Sol indicates the many hours of sunshine which the area enjoys. Behind the palm-fringed village promenade lies a small pebbled beach. On the opposite side white houses with their red roofs are clustered amongst rugged slopes with flat terracing.

The location high on the cliff above the Atlantic is spectacular. The hotel there was created by renovating an old 'quinta'. The architect responsible for the project was Tiago Oliveira. The site was also used as a vineyard. The aim was to blend an individualistic contemporary style with the original buildings and the particular surroundings. The architecture emphasises the beauty of this special spot and the relaxed atmosphere.

The hotel comprises 54 rooms, each with a balcony, divided between several buildings. A restaurant located adventurously and daringly at the cliff edge offers superb cuisine. A pool and a night bar next to the obligatory panoramic terrace represent the ideal image of a cocktail by the sea. Should the weather ever not be as perfect as in the catalogue, a perfect alternative is provided by the spa with steam saunas, Jacuzzis and all other necessary facilities.

The architecture is adapted to the cliff location with its big terracing and natural materials. The division of the rooms across several buildings has created a site that avoids being large-scale.

A light-hearted element is a steel bridge like that in a small town linking buildings across the cliff.

The interior design is modestly modern so as not to make the design a dominant feature.

Feriendorf Urnäsch

Schweiz | Switzerland   Urnäsch   Appenzellerland | Appenzell

Appenzellerstraße 11, CH-9107 Urnäsch

www.reka.ch/urnaesch, ferien@reka.ch

Tel. + 41 31 329 6699

Fertigstellung | date of completion: 2008

Architekt | architect: Dietrich Untertrifaller Architekten, A-Bregenz

Architektur | architecture: modern

Typ | accommodation: Ferienhaussiedlung | holiday houses

Einheiten | units: 50 apartments (2 1/2 - 5 1/2 Zimmer | rooms)

Das Feriendorf Urnäsch wurde von den preisgekrönten und international bekannten Architekten Dietrich/Untertrifaller und Roland Gnaiger geplant. Die Anlage, die sich in der Ostschweiz befindet, liegt in dem Dorf Urnäsch, das durch den gleichnamigen Fluss durchschnitten wird.

Die in Holzbau erstellte Anlage ist eine ganzheitliche Einheit, die alle möglichen Aktivitäten unter einem Dach vereint. Dieses Dach ist ziemlich lang, da die Anlage als Kammbebauung mit drei „Fingern" eine große Einheit bildet. Durch die Kammstruktur aber werden zwei fast geschlossene und ein offener Hofbereich gebildet, die eine kleinteiligere Atmosphäre erzeugen. An der Kantonstraße nach Appenzell steht als Schutz gegen den Verkehr ein quer gestellter Versorgungsriegel. Dieser nur eingeschossige Bau beinhaltet beispielsweise ein lang gestrecktes Schwimmbad, die Rezeption oder Gemeinschaftsräume. Ebenso umfasst die Anlage einen Kindergarten, eine Bibliothek und einen Fernsehraum. Besonderer Clou: Es werden fünf Kleintierarten in Ställen gehalten.

Die Wohnräume gehen quer zu diesem straßenseitigen Bau ab. Die Apartments sind in zweige-

schossigen Bauten eingefügt. Die Modernität der Fassaden betont das ausgereifte und umfassende Konzept modernen Urlaubs.

Insgesamt 50 Wohnungen stehen zur Verfügung. Die Zimmeranzahl reicht von zwei bis zu fünf. Die Innen-räume sind reduziert schweizerisch gestaltet. Das ab-fallende Grundstück bietet Blicke auf die begrünten Dächer der Bauwerke, da die Anlage in den Hang eingefügt ist. So integrieren sich die großen Flächen in die umliegende Natur.

Bei der Bauweise handelt es sich um einen Holzmassivbau, der nach den strikten Vorgaben der schweizerischen MINERGIE-Eco-Zertifizierung erstellt wurde. Neben den ökologischen Baumaterialien und der energieeffizienten Ausführung ist ein Blockkraft-werk zur Energieversorgung entstanden, das mit Holzschnitzeln befeuert wird.

Durch die schönen Naturmaterialien, die Hanglage und die komplexe Architektur ist so ein zeitgemäßer und vielseitiger Aufenthaltsort entstanden.

The holiday village of Urnäsch was planned by the award-winning and internationally renowned architects Dietrich/Untertrifaller and Roland Gnaiger.

The property, which is located in eastern Switzerland, lies in the village of Urnäsch, which is transacted by the river of the same name.

The wooden construction is one complete unit, bringing together all sorts of activities under one roof. This roof is quite long, as the property is a large unit layouted in the shape of a comb with three 'teeth'. The comb structure forms one open courtyard and two almost closed courtyard spaces, creating a more divided impression. On Kanton Street towards Appenzell, as a protection against traffic noise, there is an oblique long building housing various facilities. This just one-storey building houses for example a long narrow swimming pool, the reception and the communal rooms. The complex also comprises a playschool, a library and a TV room. A special feature: five types of small animals are kept in stables. The residential rooms are diagonal to this building towards the street. The apartments are incorporated into two-storey buildings. The modernity of the façades emphasises the mature and comprehensive concept of a modern holiday.

A total of 50 apartments are available. The number of rooms ranges from two to five. The interior rooms are designed in a Swiss minimalistic style. The sloped plot of land affords views over the greenery on the roofs of the buildings, as the property is embedded into the slope, thereby integrating the large surfaces into the surrounding nature.

It is a solid wood construction, built according to the strict guidelines of the Swiss MINERGIE-Eco-Label. Apart from the ecological building materials and their energy efficient implementation, a block-unit power station was developed for supplying energy, fired with wood chips. The beautiful natural materials, the sloping site and the complex architecture have created a contemporary and varied residence.

Ferienscheune

Deutschland | Germany Werneuchen/Hirschfelde Barnimer Feldmark, Brandenburg | Barnim, Brandenburg

Eduard-Arnhold-Straße 91, D-16356 Werneuchen
www.ferienscheune-barnimer-feldmark.de,
info@ferienscheune-barnimer-feldmark.de
Tel. + 49 30 3180 6684

Fertigstellung | date of completion: 2010 (Umbau | conversion)
Architekt | architect: Andreas Zerr, D-Berlin
Architektur | architecture: alt & neu | old & new
Typ | accommodation: Apartments
Einheiten | units: 5 Apartments

Die Ferienscheune Barnimer Feldmark steht in dem schönen brandenburgischen Dorf Hirschfelde. Berlin mit seinem reichhaltigen kulturellen Leben ist nur 20 km entfernt.

Eine alte, brandenburgische Feldsteinmauerscheune wurde zu fünf Wohnungen umgebaut. Die Wohnungen befinden sich im ersten Obergeschoss.
Ein großer Gemeinschaftsraum liegt im Erdgeschoss und bietet so einen direkten Kontakt zum naturbelassenen Garten. Hier finden sich eine Küche, ein großer Esstisch und ein kleiner Kaminofen.
Das Gehöft ist von schöner Natur umgeben.
Es wurden wenige Arbeiten in den Aussenbereich investiert, so dass dieser natürlich und original aussieht.

In der näheren Umgebung gibt es eine Reihe von Freizeitmöglichkeiten. So bieten die Seen Bademöglichkeiten, die Fahrradrouten Touren und die weitere Umgebung Erkundungsmöglichkeiten hinsichtlich Kultur und Kulinarischem.

The holiday barn Barnimer Feldmark is located in the beautiful Brandenburgian village of Hirschfelde. Berlin, with its rich cultural life, is only 20km away. An old Brandenburgian stone wall barn was converted into five apartments. The apartments are on the first floor. There is a large communal room on the ground floor, offering direct access to the garden which has been left untouched in a natural state. Here there is a kitchen, a large dining table and a small wood burning stove.

The homestead is surrounded by beautiful nature. Little work was invested in the outdoor spaces, and so these have retained their natural and original appearance.

In the immediate vicinity there are many leisure-time possibilities. The lakes offer swimming, the cycle routes provide tours and the further surroundings offer possibilities to explore culture and culinary arts.

Forsthaus

Deutschland | Germany   Ramsen   Naturpark Pfälzerwald | Palatinate Forest Nature Park

Eiswoog, D-67305 Ramsen
www.haeckenhaus.de

Fertigstellung | date of completion: 2010
Architekt | architect: Naumann Architektur, D-Stuttgart
Architektur | architecture: alt & neu | old & new
Typ | accommodation: Hotel
Einheiten | units: 8 Zimmer | rooms (weitere im benachbartem
            Haupthaus "Haeckenhaus" | more rooms in the
            main building 'Haeckenhaus')

Das Seehaus Forelle ist seit langem ein Ausflugslokal in Ramsen im Pfälzer Wald am See Eiswogg. Seitdem der Hotelier Jörg Maier das Haus übernommen hat, ist bereits in Zusammenarbeit mir dem Architektenpaar Naumann aus Stuttgart der Hotelanbau Haeckerhaus und der Veranstaltungspavillon „Schaustall" entstanden.

Als neueste Erweiterung ist ein benachbartes 150 Jahre altes Forsthaus hinzugekommen, das 2010 saniert wurde. Die Architekten hatten hier freie Hand und haben es geschafft, dass die Geschichte des alten Forsthauses eine Symbiose mit der neuen Nutzung als Hotel eingeht.

Es entstanden im Forsthaus acht Gästezimmer, die sich weitestgehend in die Grundstruktur des Bestandes einfügen, aber trotzdem eine eigenständige Gestaltung zeigen. Ein weiteres Zimmer befindet sich im ehemaligen Waschhaus. Das Forsthaus gibt auf den ersten Blick nach Außen wenig von den erfolgten Veränderungen preis, die Fenster sind wieder frisch gestrichen, der Sandstein leuchtet wie früher rot. Auf den zweiten Blick vermag der Besucher jedoch Hinweise auf die Veränderung zu entdecken: ES WAR EINMAL... steht auf einem um die Ecke gefaltetem Blech in Umbragrau, AUF DER LAUER an der Stützwand und DIE ERDE STILL GEKÜSST an der dem Garten zugewandten Gebäudeseite. Hinter dem Garten wurde der ehemalige Nutzgarten reaktiviert. Betritt der Besucher das Forsthaus/Hotel, so begleitet ihn das Umbragrau, der Eingang wirkt ersteinmal dunkel, doch setzten Licht Akzente auf die Zimmertüren. Der Boden ähnelt gefallenem Laub und die Treppe steht wie eine große begehbare Skulptur völlig unverändert im Flur.
Die Zimmernummern sind als Lesehilfe für die Zimmer jeweils mit einem bruchstückartigem Zitat aus einem Text beschriftet. Jedes der Gästezimmer folgt seiner eigenen kleinen Geschichte.

Die Räume sind in ihrer Grundstruktur schlicht gehalten, die Materialien wie Douglasie-Dreischichtplatten, Betonkuben, massives Eichenholz sind einfache aber „starke" Materialien. Der sparsame Einsatz von Farbe stärkt die zum Teil vom Bestand übernommenen Materialien. Die klaren kubischen Möbel sind in jedem Zimmer mit Objekten und Möbeln kontrastiert, die aus der Betriebszeit des Forsthauses stammen. So kann auch der Besucher den Bogen schlagen und seine eigenen Geschichte des Forsthauses denken.

Für den Umbau sind die Stuttgarter Architekten naumann.architektur verantwortlich. Die preisgekrönten Planer arbeiten nach dem Motto „Denn es gibt keine bedeutungslose Architektur, nur Gedankenlose."

For a long time Seehaus Forelle has been a popular tourist restaurant in Ramsen in the Pfälzer Forest at Eiswogg Lake. Since the hotelier Jörg Maier took over the building, the hotel extension and the events pavilion 'Schaustall' have been developed in cooperation with the architectural pair Naumann from Stuttgart.

A neighbouring 150-year-old forester's lodge was renovated in 2010 and added as the newest extension to the lakeside hotel Forelle in Ramsen. The architects were given free rein and managed to create a symbiosis between the history of the old forester's lodge and the new usage as a hotel.
Eight guest rooms were created in the forester's lodge, which largely conform to the basic structure of the original building but which nevertheless feature an independent design. A further room is located in the former washhouse. At first glance the forester's lodge reveals little of the implemented changes: the windows are freshly painted, the sandstone glows red like in former times. Upon closer inspection, however, the visitor can spot manifestations of the changes: ES WAR EINMAL... ('ONCE UPON A TIME...') is inscribed on an umber grey sheet of metal folded around the corner of the building, AUF DER LAUER ('ON THE LOOK-OUT') on the supporting wall and DIE ERDE STILL GEKÜSST ('GENTLY KISSED THE EARTH') on the side of the building facing the garden. Behind the garden the former kitchen garden was revitalised. Upon entering the Forester's Lodge/Hotel, the visitor is accompanied by the umber grey. The entrance appears dark at first, but light emphasises the features of the doors of the rooms. The floor looks like fallen leaves and the original unchanged stairs stand like a big walkable sculpture in the hall. To distinguish the room numbers each is inscribed with a snippet of a quotation from a literary text. Each of the guest rooms has its own little story.

The basic layout of the rooms is kept simple. The materials such as three-layer panels of Douglas fir, concrete cubes and oak wood are simple but 'solid'. The sparing use of colour emphasises the materials partly taken over from the original building. The sleek cubed furniture is contrasted in each room with objects and furniture originating from the working life of the forester's lodge, and so the visitor can establish connections and forge his own impression of the history of the forester's lodge.

The architects naumann.architektur were responsible for the conversion. The award-winning planners work according to the motto: 'For there is no meaningless architecture, only thoughtless architecture'.

Grace Santorini

Griechenland | Greece   Santorini   Insel Santorini, Ägäisches Meer | Santorini Islands, Aegean Sea

Imerovigli, GR-84700 Santorini
www.santorinigrace.com, res@santorinigrace.com
Tel. +30 22860 21300, Fax +30 22860 21299

Fertigstellung | date of completion: 2010
Architekt | architect: Divercity Architetcs, GR-Athens/UK-London
Architektur | architecture: modern
Typ | accommodation: Hotel
Einheiten | units: 20 Zimmer | rooms

Eines der spektakulärsten neuen Hotelbauten in Europa stellt das Grace Santorini dar. In der Caldera, ein geschütztes Basin, das sich durch versunkene Vulkane vor Hunderten von Jahren gebildet hat, liegt das strahlende Hotel in 300 Metern Höhe über diesem Naturwunder. Auf der gegenüberliegenden Seite liegt Skaros, berühmt für die venezianischen Burgruinen. Der Ort Imerovigli liegt auf der Ostseite der Insel und wird auch durch den Ausblick „Balkon der Ägäis" genannt.

mplusm architects, Memos Filippidis und Nicholas Travasaros von Divercity Architects, haben in drei Phasen das Aufsehen erregende Hotel geplant und bauen lassen. 2008 zeichneten sie schon verantwortlich für die Fertigstellung und die Ausstattung für die erste Phase des Neubaus. 2009/10 konnten die Architekten dann einen kompletten Neubau selbst entwerfen und haben eine faszinierende Anlage in den Hang angeschmiegt erstellen lassen. Die Grundform des Bauwerks folgt durch Knicke der

Topografie des Hangs. Die 20 Zimmer sind alle im mediterranen Weiß gehalten und sind teilweise mit dem ortstypischen schwarzen Vulkanstein versehen worden. Die Steine sind so angeordnet, dass das südliche Sonnenlicht durchdringen kann. Dieser Stein wurde ebenfalls für sichtbare Aussenmauern verwendet und kontrastiert in der hellen Sonne Griechenlands hervorragend mit dem grellen weiß.
Der Swimmingpool endet mit einer „scharfen" Kante so dass der Eindruck entsteht, es gäbe kein Becken und kein Rand. Direkt neben dem Pool befindet sich das Restaurant.

Grace Santorini is one of Europe's most spectacular new hotel buildings. The striking hotel lies at a height of 300m above the natural wonder of the Caldera, a sheltered basin that was formed hundreds of years ago by sunken volcanoes. Overlooking Skaros, famous for its Venetian castle ruins. The settlement of Imerovigli lies on the eastern side of the island and is called the 'Balcony of the Aegean' owing to its views.

Mplusm architectects, Memos Filippidis and Nicholas Travasaros from Divercity Architects, planned and built the startling hotel in three phases. 2008 saw the completion and the furnishing of the first phase of the new build.

In 2009/2010 the architects were then in charge to design a complete new building and commissioned a fascinating construction clinging to the cliff. The basic layout of the building has kinks so as to trace the cliff topography. The 20 rooms are all in Mediterranean white and are partially adorned with regional black volcanic rock. The rock is arranged in such a way that the southern sunlight can shine through. This rock was also used for conspicuous exterior walls and in the bright Greek sunshine it stands in magnificent contrast to the stark white.

The swimming pool ends with an abrupt edge, creating the impression of seamlessness. Right next to the pool is the restaurant.

Gut Sögeln

Deutschland | Germany   Bramsche bei Osnabrück   Osnabrücker Land | Osnabrück Land

An der Lindenallee 1, D-49565 Bramsche bei Osnabrück
www.gutsoegeln.de, gutsoegeln@web.de
Tel. +49 172 4322 282, Fax +49 5461 63 655

Fertigstellung | date of completion: 2008 (Umbau | conversion)
Architekt | architect: Prof. Birgit Hachtmann-Pütz, D-Hamburg
Architektur | architecture: alt & neu | old & new
Typ | accommodation: Ferienhaus | holiday house
Einheiten | units: 1 Ferienhaus mit 2 Zimmern |
1 holiday house with 2 rooms

Im Osnabrücker Land in Norddeutschland liegt das Gut Sögeln.

Erst nach einem romantischen Vorspiel, indem man über eine Brücke der Lindenallee bis zum Torturm folgt, gelangt man zu dem historischen Gut. Das von breiten Wassergräben ganz umschlossene Anwesen umfasst neben dem Haupthaus und anderen Gebäuden eine Lagerscheune. Gebaut wurde die Anlage auf mittelalterlichen Fundamenten 1793 für die Familie von Bock und Polach. Die letzte Nachfahrin, Gisela von Bock und Polach, hat die Häuser vor zwölf Jahren geerbt und aus der Gutsscheune eine exquisite Verbindung aus Tradition und Moderne geschaffen. Hier sollen geplagte Großstädter die Sorgen des Alltagslebens vergessen.
Das Entrée ziert ein weißer Kubus. Dieses gewagte Stück Innenarchitektur wurde mit der befreundeten Architektin Prof. Birgit Hachtmann-Pütz erdacht.
Die ortsansässigen Handwerker konnten mit dieser Art der Sanierung zuerst nichts anfangen. Doch durch die Verbindung von ortstypischen Baumaterialien, wie zum Beispiel Eichenholz, das aus den eigenen Wäldern stammt, mit spröden und harten Materialien wie Glas und Metall, wurden diese von dem Konzept überzeugt. Zwei elegante und moderne Zimmer sind sensibel in die alte Gebäudestruktur eingefügt. Auch hier wurden scheinbare Gegensätze, alte Möbel und klares, sachliches Inventar, genutzt. Der Respekt vor dem Bestand des Baus war so groß, dass selbst neue Steckdosen nicht in das alte Mauerwerk eingefügt wurden.

So ist ein schönes Stück Kultur weitergeschrieben worden. Und wenn Hahn Friedrich morgens kräht, kann nochmals der hoffentlich wolkenfreie norddeutsche Himmel durch die Dachfenster begutachtet werden.

The Sögeln Estate lies in the region of Osnabrück in northern Germany.

A romantic prelude leads to the historic estate, crossing a bridge and following an avenue lined with linden trees to the fortified gateway.
Apart from the main house and other buildings, the estate totally encircled by wide moats includes a barn formerly used as a storehouse. The estate was built in 1793 on medieval foundations for the family von Bock und Polach. The last descendent, Gisela von Bock und Polach, inherited the houses twelve years ago and created an exquisite combination of tradition a nd modernity out of the barn. Here stressed city dwellers can forget the worries of daily life.
The entrance is embellished with a white cube. This daring piece of interior architecture was thought out together with an architectural acquaintance Prof. Birgit Hachtmann-Pütz. The local workmen did not know what to make of this type of renovation at first. However, they were finally convinced of the concept through the combination of building materials typical of the area, such as oak wood from local forests, with brittle and hard materials such as glass and metal. Two elegant and modern rooms are incorporated respectfully into the old building structure. Here too they made use of apparent contrasts between old furniture and simple practical inventory. Respect for the original building was so great that they did not even add new electric sockets into the old walls.

In this way a beautiful piece of culture has been perpetuated. And when the cockerel crows in the morning, the hopefully cloudless north German sky can be appreciated anew through the skylights.

Hafenspeicher

Deutschland | Germany   Stralsund   Ostsee | Baltic Sea

Am Querkanal 3, D-18439 Stralsund
www.hafenspeicher-stralsund.de

Fertigstellung | date of completion: 2008 (Umbau | conversion)
Architekt | architect: Joachim Geiling, D-Stralsund
Architektur | architecture: alt & neu | old & new
Typ | accommodation: Hotel
Einheiten | units: 10 Zimmer | rooms

Masse oder Klasse? Dies war von Anfang an die entscheidende Frage bei der Entwicklung dieses Projektes. Der denkmalgeschützte Hafenspeicher wurde 1874 nach der Entfestung Stralsunds als erstes Steingebäude auf den frisch aufgeschütteten Hafeninseln für den Reeder und Händler C. A. Beug erbaut. Das neu eingefügte Hotel steht an einer der maritimsten Stellen von Stralsund, direkt am Wasser des Strelasundes, und verfügt über drei Doppelzimmer, zwei Dachsuiten, drei Maisonetteapartments und zwei Maisonettesuiten, Bistro und Bar, Aufzug, einen kleinen Wellnessbereich und eine Dachlaterne mit einem 360° Rundumblick bis Rügen.

Rotes Mauerwerk, gesandstrahlte Holzbalken, weiße Wände und Decken, erdfarbener Nadelvliesboden, Boden und Wände aus schwarzem und buntem Schiefer im Erdgeschoss, dem Saunabereich und in den Bädern, unbehandelte Grobspanplatten in der Dachuntersicht und schwarzblanker Stahl mit Rost- und Arbeitsflecken prägen die Raumeindrücke. Mit Betten, Tischen und Stühlen aus Buchenschichtholz, Schränken mit Spiegeltüren oder Birkenfurnier wird bewusst auf eine direkte und ungekünstelte Atmosphäre geachtet. Im Lehmsaunabereich harmonieren aus Seegras geflochtene Ruheliegen mit den lehmfarbenen Wänden und kontrastieren mit dem schwarzen Schiefer.
Die Verwendung des Materials Stahl beginnt mit der Tresenverkleidung an der Rezeption, setzt sich fort in den Geländerwangen des Treppenhauses und findet sich wieder in den Badezimmerregalen. Auch die kastenförmigen Leuchten aus naturbelassenem, handgeschöpften Papier begleiten den Gast vom Eingang bis ins Zimmer. In diesem klaren Umfeld werden Überraschungen wie kleine Sensationen empfunden. Alte, leinengewebte Getreidesäcke in Bretterrahmen bilden den einzigen Wandschmuck in den Zimmern.

Eine ehemalige Lastlukenabdeckung aus rissigem Leinen auf Holzrahmen mit mehrfachem, bröckelnden Kalkanstrich im Gastraum wird für eine monochrome Malerei gehalten und der hellholzfarbene Tresenbelag erweist sich als Steinplatte aus der Mancha. Der originelle und sehr persönliche Umbau des Speichers schafft eine schöne Umgebung, um das historische Stralsund und die Umgebung mit Rügen und Usedom zu erkunden.

Mass or class? That was the key question from the beginning over the course of the development of this project. The heritage-protected harbour warehouse was built in 1874 for the ship owner and tradesman C.A. Beug as the first stone building on the newly heaped up harbour islands, after the dismantling of the Stralsund fortifications.

The recently incorporated hotel stands in one of Stralsund's most maritime locations, right on the Strelasund waterfront. It comprises three double rooms, two attic suites, three maisonette apartments and two maisonette suites, a bistro and bar, a lift, a small wellness area and a roof lantern with 360° panoramic views as far as Rügen.

The impressions of the rooms are characterised by red brickwork, sandblasted wooden beams, white walls and ceilings, earth-coloured needlefelt floors, walls and floors made of black and colourful slate on the ground floor, in the sauna area and in the bathrooms, untreated rough clamping plates on the roof soffits and the use of bare black steel with rusty and used patches. Conscious attention is paid to creating a direct and natural atmosphere with the beds, tables and chairs made of beech laminated wood, cupboards with mirror doors or with birch veneer. In the clay sauna area loungers made of weaved seagrass are in harmony with the loam-coloured walls and stand in contrast to the black slate. The use of steel as a material starts with the panelling of the reception counter, continues with the banister in the stairwell and makes a further appearance in the bathroom shelves. The guests are guided from the entrance to the rooms by box-shaped lanterns made of natural handmade paper. In these light surroundings surprises are experienced as small sensations. Old woven linen grain sacks in wooden board frames are the only wall decorations in the rooms.

In the guest room a former hatch cover made of rough linen on a wooden frame, painted several times with a crumbly limewash coat, looks like a monochrome painting. The light wood-coloured surface of the reception counter is actually a stone slab from La Mancha.

The original and very personal attic conversion creates a beautiful environment from which to view historical Stralsund and the surroundings with Rügen and Usedom.

Haus Schwan

Deutschland | Germany   Sierksdorf   Lübecker Bucht, Ostsee | Bay of Lübeck, Baltic Sea

Tabakshof 9, D-23730 Sierksdorf
www.hausschwan.de, ferien@hausschwan.de

Fertigstellung | date of completion: 2009 (conversion)
Architekt | architect: Thomas Dierich, D-Hamburg
Architektur | architecture: alt & neu | old & new
Typ | accommodation: Ferienhaus | holiday house

Das Ferienhaus im Norden Deutschlands liegt in der Lübecker Bucht zwischen Haffkrug und Neustadt. Von Februar bis Juni 2009 wurde in nur vier Monaten Bauzeit das 1928/29 im traditionellen Ortskern des ehemaligen Fischerdorfes Sierksdorf errichtete Haus, umgebaut. Der Hamburger Architekt Thomas Dietrich hat das kleine Haus mit Ostseeblick unter Erhaltung traditioneller Elemente mit viel Liebe zum Detail umgestaltet. Das Resultat ist eine weitreichende Verjüngungskur, die den alten Charme nicht verändert hat.

Durch die Entkernung des Hauses und die Neugestaltung der Grundrisse wurden ein offener Wohn- und Essbereich, drei Schlafzimmer und zwei Bäder geschaffen. Das Dach erhielt zwei moderne zinkgedeckte Gauben, die zusätzlichen Raum schaffen und die Wohnfläche von ehemals ca. 86qm auf nun 100qm erweitern. Zusammen mit den neuen Balkonen bilden sie optisch einen diskreten Kontrast zum Bestand. Der Balkon bietet einen indirekten aber er-frischenden Ausblick aufs Meer.

Im Inneren verleihen hochwertige Materialien, wie Blaustein und Eichenholz, dezente Wandfarben und die durchdachte Einrichtung dem Haus seinen einladenden und gemütlichen Charakter. Alle Wohn-, Schlaf- und Badezimmer verfügen über Tageslicht und wurden bis ins kleinste Detail geplant und im modernen, wohnlichen Stil umgesetzt.
Komfort, harmonisches Design und die einfache und schöne Architektur machen das kleine „Haus Schwan" zum Feriendomizil für einen besonderen Strandurlaub. Die Kombination von klaren Linien mit einer nicht zu strengen Einrichtung erzeugen einen beson-deren Reiz.
Das Haus besitzt auch einen kleinen Garten, der besonders durch den kleinen Giebelanbau an Stimmung gewinnt. Durch diesen kleinen Anbau wird eine windgeschützte Terrasse gebildet, die bei sonnigen Tagen herrlich-norddeutsche Sommerstimmung verbreitet.

This holiday house lies northern Germany in the Bay of Lübeck between Haffkrug and Neustadt. The house was built in 1928-1929 in the traditional centre of the former fishing village of Sierksdorf and was converted in just four months from February to June 2009. The architect Thomas Dietrich from Hamburg converted the small house with views of the Baltic Sea, preserving traditional elements and paying a lot of attention to detail.

The result is a comprehensive rejuvenation which has not diminished its old charm.
Gutting the house and newly designing the layout created an open living and dining area, three bedrooms and two bathrooms. Two modern zinc-covered dormers were added to the roof, creating additional space and extending the living area from about 86m² to 100m². Together with the new balconies they form an optically discrete contrast to the original building. The balcony offers a rather indirect but refreshing view of the sea.
The interior of the house enjoys an inviting and cosy

charm, through its use of high-class materials such as blue limestone and oak wood, as well as the modest wall colours and thoughtful furnishing. All living rooms, bedrooms and bathrooms are bathed in daylight, were planned carefully down to the last detail and realised in a modern homely style.

Comfort, harmonious design and the simple and beautiful architecture make the little 'Haus Schwan' ('Swan House'), just 30m from the Baltic Sea shore, a holiday residence promising a special beach holiday. The combination of clear lines with casual furnishings lends it its particular charm.
The house also has a garden, whose atmosphere is enhanced by a small gabled building extension. This extension forms a terrace sheltered from the wind, exuding a wonderfully northern German summer atmosphere on sunny days.

Hidden Hotel

Frankreich | France   Paris   Paris Innenstadt | Paris city

28, Rue de l'Arc Triomphe, FR-75017 Paris
www.hiden-hotel.com, contact@hidden-hotel.com
Tel. + 33 0140 55 03 57, Fax +33 0145 74 45 87

Fertigstellung | date of completion: 2009
Architekt | architect: Interieur by Hidden Cabin, FR-Paris
Architektur | architecture: modern
Typ | accommodation: Hotel
Einheiten | units: 23 Zimmer | rooms

Im Herzen von Paris ist ein versteckter und geheimnisvoller Ort entstanden. Allzugroße Sorgnis sollte man aber nicht haben. Immerhin handelt es sich ja um ein Hotel. Nur hat das Hidden Hotel das Versteckte und die Überraschung zu seinem Leitthema gemacht. Eine schöne Idee, da eine historische Metropole wie Paris viele Orte zum Entdecken bereithält. Warum dann nicht auch ein Hotel mit gehobenem Anspruch?

Das Hotel liegt nahe dem Arc de Triomphe in der gleichnamigen Straße. In einem Altbau hat sich das Hotel regelrecht eingenistet. Die massive Holztür deutet schon an, dass hier Ruhe und Entspannung herrschen soll. Die dunkle Fassade unterstützt den Eindruck des Verborgenen.
Der Empfang ist in gedämpftes Licht getaucht. Edelste Materialien umgebend das Interieur. Elegante dunkle Töne verbreiten einen luxuriöses Ambiente.

Ein kleiner Garten verbindet den Frühstücksraum mit dem Aussenraum. Auch hier kann sich zurück gezogen werden. Eine Küche im Erdgeschoss mit Sitzgelegenheiten für 12 Personen kann gemietet werden. Des Weiteren bietet eine kleine Bar einen urbanen Ort für Cocktails.

Das Haus hat 23 Gästezimmer auf sechs Pariser Stockwerken. Diese sind zwischen 14 und 25 m² groß und sind mit sinnlichen Materialien und warmen Licht ausgestattet. Kontrastiert wird dieses durch unbehandelte Oberflächen wie beispielsweise Holzfussböden.

A hidden and mysterious spot has been created in the heart of Paris. But this should not be a great cause for speculation as it is merely a hotel, it is just that the Hidden Hotel has made clandestinity and the unexpected its key theme. This is a great idea, as a historical metropolis like Paris holds many places to discover. So why not also have a hotel with sophisticated aspirations?

The hotel lies near the Arc de Triomphe in the street of the same name. The hotel is nestled into an old building. The solid wooden door already indicates that peace and relaxation reign supreme here. The dark façade reinforces the impression of secrecy.
The entrance is bathed in dim light. Upscale materials adorn the interior. Elegant dark tones diffuse a luxurious atmosphere.

A small garden links the breakfast room with the exterior, to which one can also retreat. One can rent a kitchen on the ground floor which seats 12 people. Furthermore a small bar provides an urban area for enjoying cocktails.

The house has 23 guest rooms on six Parisian floors. These are between 14m² and 25m² in size and are characterised by sensual materials and warm light. These are contrasted with natural surfaces like the wooden floorboards.

Holländerhaus

Deutschland | Germany   Potsdam   Potsdam Innenstadt | Potsdam city

Kurfürstenstraße 15, D-14476 Potsdam
www.hollaenderhaus-potsdam.de, hollaenderhaus@potsdam.de
Tel. +49 331 279 11 0, Fax +49 331 27911 1

Fertigstellung | date of completion: 1994 (Umbau | conversion)
Architekt | architect: Siegfried Polaczy, D-Berlin + Dagmar Marx,
                                    D-Reutlingen & Harald Dieckmann, D-Potsdam
Architektur | architecture: alt & neu | alt & neu
Typ | accommodation: Apartments
Einheiten | units: 10 Apartments

Das Apartmenthotel liegt im historischen holländischen Viertel der Landeshauptstadt Brandenburgs, Potsdam. Die Stadt gehört zum Weltkulturerbe der UNESCO und dieses gilt insbesondere für das historische holländische Viertel.
Das Stadtviertel ist ab 1733 durch den holländischen Baumeister Boumann entstanden. Es umfasst 134 Häuser, die alle in rotem Backstein erstellt wurden. Sinn und Zweck des Viertels war, niederländische Handwerker in die preußische Provinz zu locken.

Das kleine Apartmenthotel in der Kurfürstenstraße ist ein giebelständiges Bauwerk aus dieser Zeit. Mit seinen schönen Proportionen und weißen Stucklineaturen erweckt es die Stimmung der Grachtenstädte an der Nordsee.
Auch hier wurde die Moderne mit der Tradition originell verbunden. Moderne Einbauten teilen neue Nutzungen wie Bäder ab. Diese, wie eingestellte Kuben gestaltet, kontrastieren hervorragend mit dem alten Bauwerk. Selbst technische Installationen, wie ein freischwebendes Metallgestell zur Positionierung des Fernsehers, erwecken die Assoziation zu den alten, außen liegenden Seilzügen der Handwerkerhäuser.
Eine kleine Küche ist Grundlage für die Bewirtung von Frühstücksgästen im Innenhof, Wintergarten oder im Frühstücksraum. Gute Restaurants bietet die unmittelbare Nachbarschaft im Holländischen Viertel. Ein Minifitnessraum dient zum Abbau der Restenergie, soweit diese nicht zur Erkundung der romantischen und überwältigenden Erscheinung der Stadt Potsdam verausgabt wurde.

Ein kleiner Garten kann im Sommer als lauschiger Essplatz genutzt werden.
Für längere Aufenthalte bietet das Haus gute Voraussetzungen mit Spezialpreisen ab 1 Woche bzw. 1 Monat sowie in einigen Apartments sehr gute Arbeitsbedingungen.
Neben zwei klassischen 2 ½ -stöckigen Giebelhäusern stehen für die Apartments mehrere Hofgebäude bereit, die zwischen 1890 und 1900 erbaut wurden. In dieser Zeit ist auch das barocke Vorderhaus komplett überformt und reichhaltig mit Schmuckelementen versehen worden.

Die beteiligten Architekten waren Siegfried Polaszy aus Berlin, Dagmar Marx aus Reutlingen für die Innenraumgestaltung und Harald Dieckmann aus Potsdam (Bauherr und Architekt).

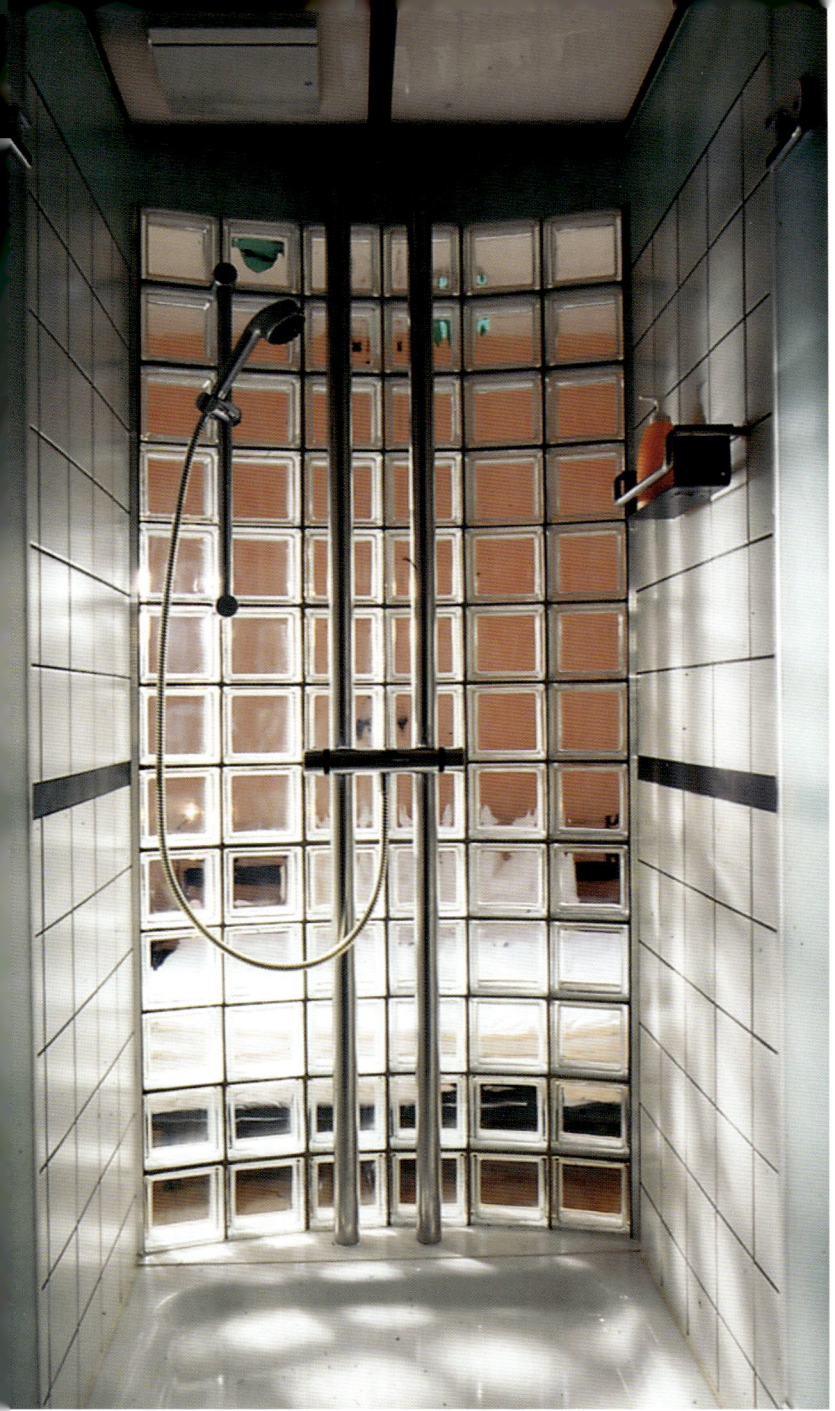

The aparthotel lies in the historic Dutch quarter of Potsdam, the regional capital of Brandenburg. The city is a UNESCO World Heritage site, particularly the historic Dutch quarter. This city district was developed from 1733 by the Dutch master builder Boumann. It comprises 134 houses all built in red bakestone. The purpose of the district was to entice Dutch craftsmen to the Prussian province.

The small aparthotel on Kurfürsten Street is a gabled building originating during those times. With its beautiful proportions and white stucco geometric lines it recreates the atmosphere of the canal towns by the North Sea. Modern and traditional elements were combined in an original way. Modern additions provide new facilities such as bathrooms. These,

designed as inserted cubes, contrast splendidly with the old building. Even technical installations, like a free-standing metal frame for positioning the television, are reminiscent of the old rope hoists on the outside of the artisans' houses.

A small kitchen is the base for catering for breakfast guests in the interior courtyard, conservatory or the breakfast room. Good restaurants are available in the immediate vicinity of the Dutch quarter. One can expend any excess energy in the mini fitness room, whatever is left after exploring the romantic and overwhelming experience of the town of Potsdam. A small garden can be used in summer as a cosy dining area.

The house offers good deals for longer stays with special prices starting from a week or a month, and some apartments also have very good conditions for working.

Apart from two classical 2 ½ storey gabled houses, several courtyard buildings also provide further apartments, built between 1890 and 1900. During this period the baroque front house was also completely reformed and lavish decorative elements were added.

The participating architects were Siegfried Polaszy from Berlin, Dagmar Marx from Reutlingen for the interior design and Harald Dieckmann from Potsdam (building owner and architect).

Das Ferienhaus als Grand Hotel

Nein, der ideale Kandidat, um dem architektonisch anspruchsvollen Ferienhaus eine Hommage zu verfassen, bin ich nicht. Beziehungsweise: war ich nicht. Das hat sich allerdings geändert, was mit meiner kleinen Tochter Marie und einem iranischen Taxifahrer zusammenhängt. Ich komme darauf gleich zurück.

Vorab: Als Architekturkritiker mag ich womöglich in Betracht kommen, um das architektonisch Anspruchsvolle an sich zu würdigen – aber auch das architektonisch anspruchsvolle Ferienhaus? Müsste man dazu nicht ein großer Freund auch des Ferienhauses an sich sein? Hm, nun . . . sagen wir so: Aus dem Stand könnte ich zumindest sein Gegenstück, das Grand Hotel, als bedeutendste Errungenschaft der Zivilisation lobpreisen, sei es das Baur au Lac in Zürich (die Halle!) das Imperial in Wien (der Butler Service!), das Victoria-Jungfrau in Interlaken (das Sensai Select Spa!) oder auch den Bayerischen Hof in München, in dessen Bar die Cocktailkarte ausdrücklich darauf hinweist, dass vom „Zombie" allerhöchstens zwei Gläser serviert werden. Nicht, dass ich mich hier als Zombie-Fan outen will, aber für gefährlich klingende Cocktailkarten, raumverschwenderische Hallen, zuvorkommende Butler oder angenehme Spa-Träume bin ich empfänglich. Grand Hotels, finde ich, wie der Name schon sagt, nahezu großartig.

Das Beste daran: In solchen Hotels kann man immer ein bisschen so tun, als wäre man jemand anderes. Man kann sich für wenige Stunden in gewisser Weise neu erfinden – und manchmal erfindet man sich die dandyhafte Noblesse des 19. Jahrhunderts gleich mit dazu. (Und wer sich jetzt fragt, was das alles mit Ferienhäusern zu tun habe, dem muss an dieser Stelle die dandyhafte Noblesse antworten: nur Geduld!)

Vorher ist noch die Sache mit Marie zu klären. Vor einigen Jahren war ich aus beruflichen Gründen in Berlin. Mit dabei war meine kleine Marie. Wir wohnten im Regent. Wer das Regent kennt, der weiß, dass es dort ein ausgezeichnetes Restaurant gibt, das in den Vormittagsstunden für das Frühstück genutzt wird. Weil dort aber, nicht unüblich in großen Häusern, eine gewisse steife Manierlichkeit herrscht, habe ich meiner heute 12-jährigen Tochter, sie war damals vielleicht fünf Jahre alt, eingeschärft, sie müsse sich „ordentlich benehmen". Bei uns zuhause sah der Frühstückstisch, sobald ihn Marie verließ, nämlich immer so aus, als müsste er vom Gesundheitsamt und/oder vom Technischen Hilfswerk wegen dringender Aufräumarbeiten gesperrt werden. Marie saß daher schwer verschüchtert und kerzengerade im Regent zu Tisch, rührte weder Obstsalat noch Bircher Müsli an, behauptete, nein danke, man habe keinen Hunger, äh Appetit, verneinte sogar das Kakao-Angebot und bat lediglich um ein Glas höchst stillen Wassers. Aber auch da hatte sie Angst, sie könnte etwas verschütten. Als wir das Taxi zum Flughafen bestiegen, hatte sie praktisch nicht gefrühstückt, weshalb ihr und ihrem lautstark knurrenden Magen kurz vor dem Flughafen Tegel vom sympathischen iranischen Taxifahrer ein Croissant angeboten wurde. Aus einer Tüte mit drei Croissants bediente sie sich so gierig, dass nichts übrig blieb. Der sympathische iranische Taxifahrer blickte mich im Rückspiegel sehr lange an. Wahrscheinlich überlegte er, ob es zur deutschen Leitkultur gehört, kleine blonde Mädchen hungern zu lassen.

Was lernen wir daraus? Grand Hotels sind per se großartig, aber von Fall zu Fall können sie auch anstrengend sein. Ja, endlich, das (und die Tatsache, dass sich zu Marie bald noch zwei kleine Brüder gesellten) führt nun zum Ferienhaus. Ich bin nicht mehr sicher, ob das davor oder nachdem war. Davor oder nachdem Lelo, der Hool der Familie, seinen etwas älteren Bruder

Mauritz dazu animierte, in einem anderen großen Hotel den Feueralarm zu betätigen. Ich schätze: Es war danach.

Jedenfalls verbringen wir seither alle Ferien in einem sogenannten Ferienhaus. Gegen meinen Willen, aber im Interesse einer gewissen robusten Familien-Gemütlichkeit. Das ist nämlich einerseits das Tolle an den (üblichen) Ferienhäusern: Man lebt dort ganz wie zuhause. Es wird lärmend gefrühstückt, der Tisch wird verwüstet, dann wird abgespült – und die Badehosen hängen zum Trocknen an irgendwelchen Stuhllehnen. Weil das die meisten Besitzer von Ferienhäusern wissen, möblieren sie die Ferienhäuser ausschließlich mit Billigmöbeln, die nach zwei Jahren schon so aussehen, als hätte man mit ihnen ein langes, langes Leben vorzugsweise in bürgerkriegsähnlichen Verhältnissen verbracht. Und das ist auch das Schlimme an den (üblichen) Ferienhäusern: Man kann ihn ihnen wunderbar das eigene robuste, ganz normale, gewohnte Zuhause nachspielen, man kann sich aber darin meist nicht so gut neuerfinden – sei es als Schlossherr, Dandy oder verwöhnter Snob.

Und Ferien sind doch definitiv die beste Gelegenheit, auch mal Ferien vom eigenen, leider wahren Ich zu machen, nicht wahr? Aber das nun führt schließlich doch noch zur Hommage an jene absolut unüblichen Ferienhäuser, die in diesem Buch versammelt sind: Sie sind die Schnittstelle aus Grand Hotel, neuerfundenem Ich und Marie-Mauritz-Lelo-tauglicher Familien-Lässigkeit. Jetzt müsste sich meine liebe Ehefrau nur noch dazu bereit erklären, den imperialen Butler Service zu übernehmen, dann wollte ich nie mehr anderswo leben. Ein größeres Kompliment an architektonisch ambitionierte Ferienhäuser, die nicht nur behaglich, sondern auch großartig sind, die nicht nur authentisch sind, sondern auch als fabelhafte Kulissen für surreale Sehnsuchtsmomente der puren Eleganz dienen: fällt mir beim besten Willen nicht ein.

Gerhard Matzig wurde 1963 in Deggendorf geboren und studierte Jura, Politik und Architektur in Bochum, Passau und München. Heute lebt Matzig mit seiner Familie in der Nähe von München, wo er für die *Süddeutsche Zeitung* tätig ist. Er begann dort im Feuilleton als zuständiger Redakteur für Architektur und Städtebau. Seit 2009 ist er Leiter des Ressorts *„SZ Wochenende"*. Für seine journalistische Tätigkeit in den Bereichen Architektur und Design wurde er mit zahlreichen renommierten Preisen geehrt.

The Holiday Home as Grand Hotel

No, I am not the ideal candidate to compose a homage to architecturally sophisticated holiday homes. Or rather: I wasn't. However, that has changed, owing to my little daughter Marie and an Iranian taxi driver. I will come back to that shortly.

Let's start by saying that I might not be considered as an architecture critic in a position to pay tribute to architectural qualities in themselves- let alone architecturally appealing holiday homes. Wouldn't one also need to be a big fan of holiday homes for that? Hmm, well...let's put it like this: offhand I could at least sing the praises of its counterpart, the grand hotel, as the most significant achievement of civilisation, whether it is the Baur in Zürich (the hall!), the Imperial in Vienna (the butler service!) , the Victoria-Jungfrau in Interlaken (the Sensei Select Spa!) or also the Bayerischer Hof in Munich, whose cocktail menu in the bar specifically indicates that no more than two glasses of 'Zombie' will be served. Not that I want to reveal myself as a Zombie fan here, but I am susceptible to dangerous-sounding cocktail menus, excessively vast halls, courteous butlers and pleasant spa dreams. I find grand hotels, as the name already suggests, simply grandiose.

The best thing about such hotels is that one can always pretend a little to be someone else. For a few hours one can sort of reinvent oneself, and sometimes one can play at 19th century dandyish noblesse at the same time. (And for those who are asking themselves right now what all this has to do with holiday homes, the answer at this point from the dandyish noblesse has to be: just be patient!)

Before that let me explain the thing about Marie. A few years ago I was in Berlin for work. My little Marie was with me. We were staying at the Regent. Whoever knows the Regent is aware that it boasts an excellent restaurant, which is used for breakfast in the morning. However, because there was a certain stiff adherence to manners, as is quite typical of large hotels, I reminded my now 12-year-old daughter , then just five, that she had to 'behave decently'. For at home our breakfast table, as soon as Marie left it, always looked like it should be closed off by the health ministry and/or the technical emergency service for urgent clean-up operations. And so Marie was sitting there very shyly and bolt upright at the table in the Regent, not touching the fruit salad or the Bircher muesli, claiming no thank you, she was not hungry or rather had no appetite, even refusing the offer of cocoa and asking for just a glass of very still water. But even then she was still afraid she might spill something. When we got into the taxi to the airport she had hardly eaten any breakfast, which is why just before Tegel airport she and her loudly rumbling tummy were offered a croissant by the amenable Iranian taxi driver. She helped herself so greedily from the bag of three croissants that none were left. The nice Iranian taxi driver looked at me at length in the rear view mirror. He was probably wondering whether it was part of German mainstream culture to let little blonde girls go hungry.

What lessons can we draw from this? Grand hotels are splendid per se, but in some cases they can be tiring too. Yes and this (and the fact that two little brothers were soon to join Marie), finally leads me to holiday homes. I am not sure anymore whether that was before or after. Before or after Lelo, the cheeky monkey of the family, egged his slightly older brother Mauritz on to set off the fire alarm in another large hotel. I reckon it was after that.

In any case since then we spend all holidays in so-called holiday homes. Against my will, but in the interests of a certain dependable family cosiness. For that is on the one hand the great thing about typical holiday homes: one lives there just like at home. One can have noisy breakfasts, the table looks like a bomb has hit it, and then there's the washing up – and the swimming trunks are hung up to dry somewhere on the arms of chairs. As most owners of holiday homes are aware of this, they furnish them exclusively with cheap furniture, which two years on already looks like it has been put through a long long life primarily in civil war-like conditions. And that is also the worst thing about typical holiday homes: one can imitate wonderfully one's own solid, quite normal and habitual home life, but most of the time they do not lend themselves very well to reinventing oneself – whether it is the lord of the manor, dandy or spoilt snob.

However, holidays are definitely the best opportunity to also take a holiday from one's own and unfortunately true self, are they not? Finally this leads after all to the homage to those absolutely untypical holiday homes collected in this book: they are at the meeting point of grand hotel, reinvented self and Marie-Mauritz-Lelo

casual family suitability. Now my dear wife just has to say she is prepared to take over the Imperial butler service, then I would never want to live anywhere else. I truly can not think of a greater compliment I could pay to architecturally ambitious holiday homes, which are not only cosy but also splendid, not only authentic but also serve as a fabulous backdrop to surreal moments of longing for pure elegance.

Gerhard Matzig was born in Deggendorf in 1963 and studied law, political science and architecture in Bochum, Passau and Munich. He lives with his family on the outskirts of Munich. He works for the *Süddeutsche Zeitung*, initially as an editor for the features section, in particular responsible for the area of architecture and urban planning. Since 2009 he is head of the department *SZ Wochenende (SZ Weekend)*. He has been awarded renowned prizes for his journalistic activities in the areas of architecture and design.

Hopper St. Josef

Deutschland | Germany   Köln   Köln Innenstadt | Cologne City

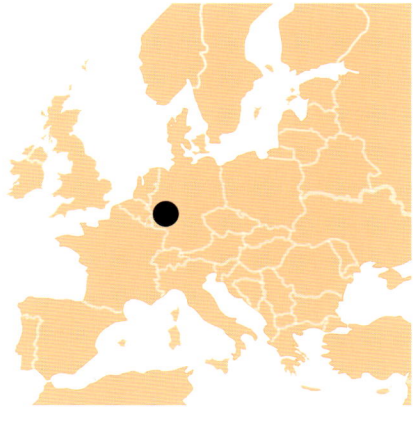

Dreikönigenstraße 1-3, D-50678 Köln
www.hopper.de, st.josef@hopper.de
Tel. +49 221 99800 0, Fax +49 221 99800 111

Fertigstellung | date of completion: 2009 (Umbau | conversion)
Architekt | architect: Rolf Kursawe, Architekten HKR, D-Köln
Architektur | architecture: alt & neu | alt & neu
Typ | accommodation: Hotel
Einheiten | units: 65 | 21 Einzel-, 44 Doppelzimmer |
21 single, 44 double

Das HOPPER Hotel St. Josef liegt ruhig und dennoch verkehrsgünstig in der Kölner Südstadt. Nur zwei Minuten zu Fuß entfernt liegen Rhein und Rheinauhafen einerseits und die belebte Severinstraße andererseits. Über diese erreicht man zu Fuß die Innenstadt mit dem am Dom gelegenen Hauptbahnhof innerhalb von 15-20 Minuten.

2009 wurde das St. Josef als das dritte Hotel in der Reihe der Hopper-Familie eröffnet. Das neue Hotel wurde in das alte „St. Josefs-Haus der Pfarre St. Severin" eingefügt. Das Haus hat eine bewegte Geschichte. 1891 wurde das Bauwerk im „Arme-Leute-Viertel" als „Kleinkinderbewahrschule" gegründet. Später zogen weitere Nutzungen zur Finanzierung der erweiterten karitativen Maßnahmen, wie Speisung von armen Schulkindern, eine Handarbeitsschule für junge Mädchen sowie ein Heim für junge Frauen, in das Haus ein. Im zweiten Weltkrieg wurde der Bau stark zerstört, doch konnte der Großteil der Substanz gerettet werden. 2006 zogen langsam die letzten Nutzungen, wie beispielsweise ein Kindergarten, aus.

Ziel des Konzeptes war es, in Planung und Umsetzung ein fortschrittliches Gastgeben zu verwirklichen, das den Gedanken der ehemaligen Nutzung aufgreift und sich auf das Wesentliche in Form und Funktion konzentriert. Verzicht auf alles übliche Überflüssige vieler Hotelkonzepte war der Grundgedanke.
Einzel- und Doppelzimmer stehen in verschiedenen Größen und wahlweise mit schmalem oder breitem Bett zur Verfügung. Die Zimmer verfügen teilweise über Klimaanlage, einen eigenen kleinen Balkon und eine Verbindungstür.

Das Gestaltungsprinzip passt sich der modern-zurückhaltenden Einrichtung an. Zeitgenössische Interpretationen der St. Josef-Skulptur des Eingangsportals sind das begleitende Thema in den Zimmern. Im Erdgeschossbereich befinden sich eine modern-gemütliche Bar und eine Bibliothek mit Kamin. Eine besondere Atmosphäre bietet das in die alte Kapelle eingebaute Restaurant. Der zweigeschossige Raum wurde original wieder hergestellt. Hier wurden der originale Parkettboden und die Wandmalereien erhalten. Die Küche bietet eine Auswahl an internationalen Gerichten.

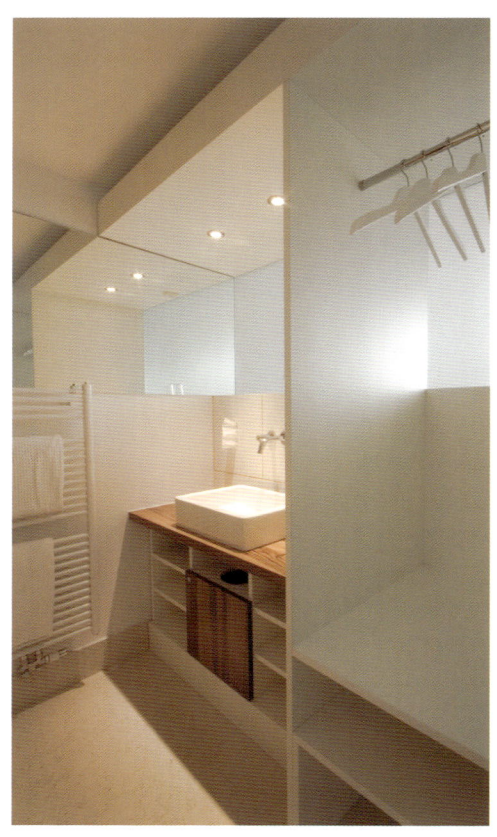

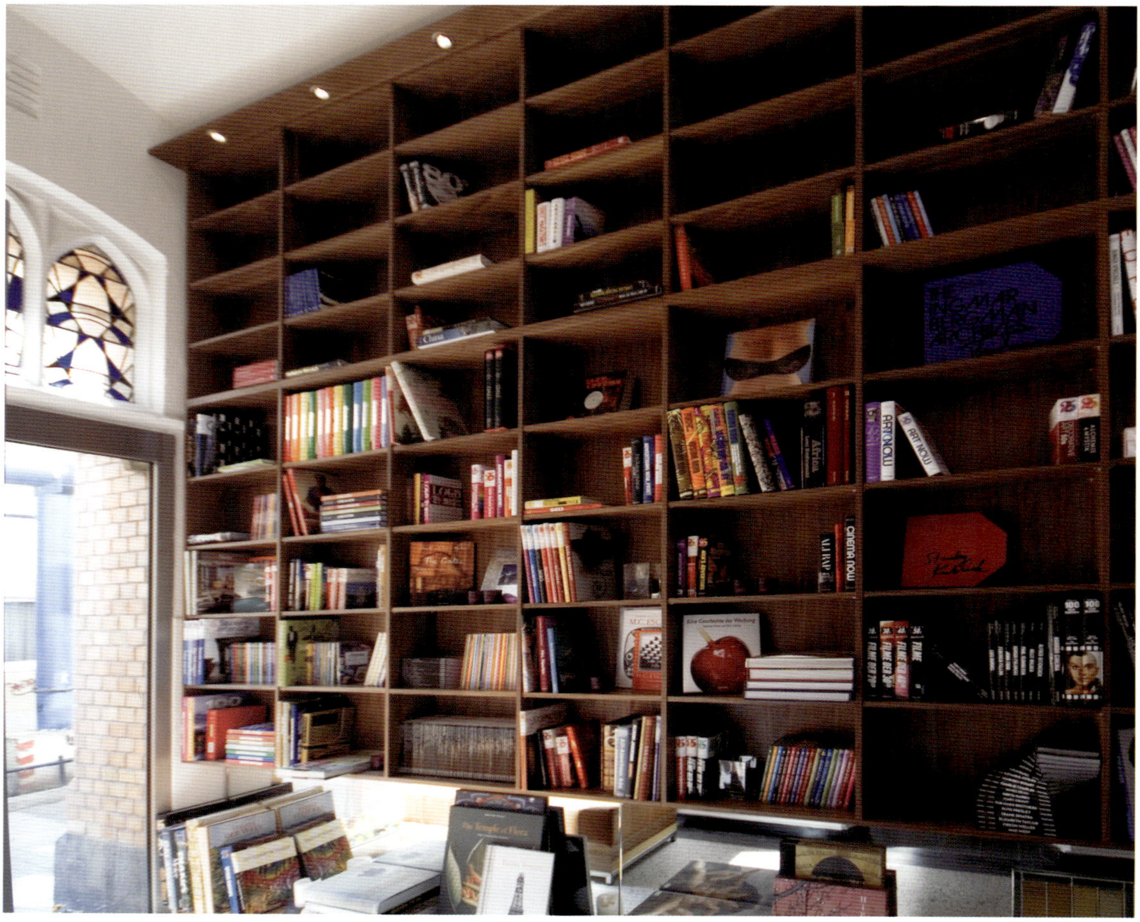

ART NOW
Africa
cinema now
Eine Geschichte der Werbung
The Temple of Flora

The hotel Hopper St. Josef lies in a quiet but nevertheless easily accessible location in the south of Cologne. Just two minutes away on foot are the Rhine and the harbour and also the lively Severin Street, which leads within a 15-20 minute walk to the city centre with the main station near the Cathedral.

In 2009 St. Josef was opened as the third hotel in the chain created by the Hopper family was opened. The new hotel was incorporated into the old 'St. Josef's House of the St. Severin Parish'. The house has an eventful history. In 1891 the building was founded in the 'poor people's district' as a nursery for small children. Later other functions moved into the house to finance the charitable initiatives, such as the feeding of poor school children, a needlework school for young girls, and a hostel for young women. In World War II the building was badly damaged, but the majority of the original building could be redeemed. In 2006 the last of the occupiers, such as a kindergarten, moved out.

The aim of the concept was to plan and implement a forward-looking hosting of guests, which echoes the spirit of the original usage of the building and concentrates on the essentials in form and function. The fundamental principle was to refrain from all the usual superfluous elements of many hotel concepts. Single and double rooms in different sizes are available, either with a narrow or a wide bed. Some of the rooms have air conditioning, their own balcony and a connecting door.

The design principle adheres to modern and discrete furnishing. Contemporary interpretations of the St Josef sculpture in the entrance portal are the accompanying theme in the rooms.
On the ground floor there is a modern and cosy bar and a library with a fireplace.
The restaurant built into the old chapel offers a special atmosphere. The two-storey space incorporates and preserves many original features, such as the original parquet floor and the wall paintings. The kitchen offers a range of international dishes.

Hotel Aire de Bardenas

Spanien | Spain   Tudela   Navarra, Ebrotal | Navarre, Ebro valley

Ctra. de Ejea, Km. 1,5, ES-31500 Tudela
www.airedebardenas.com | indo@hotelaire.com
Tel. +34 948 11 66 66, Fax +34 948 11 63 48

Fertigstellung | date of completion: 2007
Architekt | architect: E. Milano Lopez & M. Rivera, ES-Barcelona
Architektur | architecture: modern
Typ | accomodation: Hotel
Einheiten | units: 22 Zimmer | rooms

Am Rande des Naturparks Bardenas Reales, einer
einzigartigen Halbwüstenlandschaft Spaniens,
befindet sich unweit der Stadt Tudela das vier Sterne
Hotel Aire de Bardenas.

Von außen wirkt der Komplex mit seinen manns-
hohen Palisaden aus gestapelten Obst- und Gemüse-
holzkisten und den metallenen Boxen zuerst kurios.
Doch der Rückgriff auf hier überall anzutreffende
Elemente ist bewusst gewählt. Zum einem suchen die
Architekten Emiliano Lopez und Monica Rivera stets
eine Verbindung zum kulturellen- und landschaft-
lichen Kontext herzustellen, zum anderen benutzten
sie diese „Readymades" als effektive und kosten-
günstige Bauelemente, die einfach zu montieren sind
und gegen Einblicke und den hier häufig auftretenden
Nordwestwind schützen.
Dieser Wüstenwind gab neben dem Namen des
Hotels auch den Ausschlag für die Konzeption einer
kleinen Wohnstadt aus insgesamt 22 einzeln er-
schlossenen Wohneinheiten, die teilweise über einen
eigenen Außenbereich verfügen. Ihre Verteilung über
das Gelände ist so gewählt, das spannende Zwischen-
räume Ausblicke und windgeschützte Privatbereiche
ausbilden. Organisiert wird der Komplex über einen
zentralen Patio, der windgeschützt die Gemeinschafts-
bereiche wie Rezeption, Restaurant und den Hotelpool
beherbergt. Von dort gehen die einzelnen Erschlie-
ßungswege zu den jeweiligen Wohneinheiten. Alle
Gebäude sind in Anlehnung an die lokale Funktions-
architektur in einer schlichten kubischen Form gehalten.
Als Bauweise wurde aufgrund eines engen Kosten-
rahmens und einer kurzen Fertigstellungfrist von nur
12 Monaten eine einfach zu montierende Stahlkonstruktion mit einer Wärmedämmfassade aus
Aluminiumsandwichpanelen ausgeführt.
Die Außenanlagen wurden ebenso bewusst aus orts-
üblicher Vegetation und Materialen angelegt, um eine
möglichst enge Verbindung mit der kargen Landschaft herzustellen.

Eine weitere Besonderheit stellen die großflächigen
Fensteröffnungen dar, die den Blick auf die wüsten-
artige Landschaft freigeben. Sie sind in Form aus-
kragender Kästen ausgebildet und fungieren als eine
Art „Aussichtssofa". In der Fensterleibung befindet sich
übrigens der obligatorische Hotelfernseher, wobei die
Blickwahl nicht schwer fallen sollte.

At the edge of the nature preserve of Bardenas Reales, a unique semi-desert landscape in Spain, lies the 4-star Hotel Aire de Bardenas near the town of Tudela.

The exterior of the complex with its head-high palisades made of stacked wooden fruit and vegetable crates and metal boxes creates a curious impression at first. But the resorting to elements typical of the area is a deliberate choice. Firstly the architects Emiliano Lopez and Monica Rivera are constantly seeking to establish connections to the context of the culture and landscape, and secondly they used these 'readymades' as effective and economical building elements, which are easy to assemble and serve as a shield against being overlooked as well as against the frequent northwesterly wind.
This desert wind not only gave the hotel its name but was also a decisive factor behind the concept of a small residential town consisting of 22 individual housing units, some of which have their own outdoors space. Their distribution across the site is selected so that interesting spaces in between provide views and private areas sheltered from the wind.
The complex is organised around a central patio, which is sheltered from the wind and houses the communal areas such as the reception, restaurant and hotel pool. From there individual paths lead to the respective accommodation units. All the buildings are in a simple cubed form, in accordance with the local functional architecture. Owing to the tight budget and a short completion term of just 12 months, the chosen building materials were an easy to mount steel construction with an insulated façade made of aluminium sandwich panels.
The outside space was equally consciously laid out with regional vegetation and materials, to create as close a connection as possible with the barren landscape.

The large-scale window openings are a further feature, affording open views towards the desert-like landscape. They are in the form of protruding boxes and act as a sort of 'viewing sofa'. The obligatory hotel TV is in the window space, although one's choice of views shouldn't be difficult.

Hotel Alpina

Schweiz | Switzerland   Vals   Graubünden, Valsertal | Grisons, Valservalley

CH-7132 Vals-Valsertal
www.hotel-alpina-vals.ch, info@hotel-alpina-vals.ch
Tel. +41 81 920 70 40, Fax +41 81 920 40 41

Fertigstellung | date of completion: 2006
Architekt | architect: Gion A. Caminada, CH-Vrin
Architektur | architecture: alt & neu | alt & neu
Typ | accommodation: Hotel
Einheiten | units: 12 Zimmer | rooms

Das Hotel Alpina in Vals befindet sich seit 1930 in Familienbesitz und wird bereits in dritter Generation von der Familie Kühne geführt. In seinem Kern ist das Haus über 100 Jahre alt und hat sein Gesicht im Verlauf dieser Jahre durch folgenreiche Umbauten mehrmals verändert. 2001 wurde der Architekt Gion Caminada, Professor an der ETH Zürich und Vorbild einer gesamten Generation von Architekten mit hohem Anspruch, mit der Neugestaltung der Fassade, dem Eingangsbereich mit Empfang und Speisesaal beauftragt. Zusätzlich entstanden drei spezielle Zimmer mit Sitzerkern. 2006 wurden weitere Zimmer in der zweiten und dritten Etage revitalisiert und im Jahre 2008 nahm sich der Architekt auch noch der dritten Umbauetappe, der Bargestaltung, an.

Neben der berühmten Therme Vals, die von dem international bekannten Architekten Peter Zumthor gebaut wurde und so zum Pilgerziel von Architekten und Wellness-Begeisterten geworden ist, zeigt auch das Alpina, dass zeitgemäße, sensibel gestaltete Bauten in historisch gewachsenen Dörfern eine Bereicherung sein können.

Nun steht das Hotel mit seinen tiefen Leibungen der Holzrahmenfenstern wie selbstverständlich direkt am Dorfplatz. Die Fassade scheint modern– und doch fügt sie sich nahezu nahtlos in das historische Umfeld mit Kirche und den Blockbauwohnhäusern ein.

Die Architektur versprüht eine dezente, edle Ausstrahlung, die es in zurückhaltender Art versteht, den Raum für sich zu gewinnen.
Im Eingangsbereich dominieren Valser-Steinplatten, Eichenholzboden und der kubische Empfangstresen. Das Speiserestaurant im ersten Stock, ebenfalls modern und in Eichenholz gehalten, hält das Gleichgewicht zwischen formeller und zwangloser Atmosphäre. Die mittlerweile zwölf neu gestalteten Gästezimmer beeindrucken mit ihrer warmen, stilvollen Schlichtheit.

Hotel Alpina in Vals has been family-owned since 1930 and is already being managed by the third generation of the Kühne family. The core of the house is over 100 years old and has changed its appearance several times over the course of the years through a series of conversions. In 2001 the architect Gion Caminada, Professor at the ETH Zurich and the role model of a whole generation of architects with high aspirations, was commissioned with redesigning the façade, the entrance area and the dining room. In addition three special rooms with seating bays were created. In 2006 further rooms on the second and third floors were revitalised and in 2008 the architect launched the third stage of the conversion, the design of the bar area.

Apart from the famous Vals spa, built by the internationally renowned architect Peter Zumthor and becoming a pilgrimage destination for architects and wellness enthusiasts, the Alpina also shows that contemporary and thoughtfully designed buildings can be an asset to historical villages.

Now the hotel, with its deeply recessed wooden framed windows, stands directly on the village square. The façade appears modern- but nevertheless it is integrated almost seamlessly into the historical surroundings with the church and the apartment blocks. The architecture has a discrete and noble presence, establishing its presence in a modest way.
The entrance area is dominated by Vals stone slabs, oak floorboards and the cubed reception counter. The restaurant on the first floor, also modern and with oak, maintains the balance between a formal and casual atmosphere. The twelve newly designed guest rooms have an impressive and warm stylish elegance.

Hotel Hinteregger

Österreich | Austria   Matrei i. Osttirol   Tirol | Tyrol

Hintermarkt 4, A-9971 Matrei i. Osttirol
www.hinteregger.at, hotel.hinteregger@netway.at
Tel. +43 4875 6587, Fax +43 4875 65877

Fertigstellung | date of completion: 2007
Architekt | architect: Madritsch/Pfurtscheller, A-Innsbruck
Architektur | architecture: alt & neu, modern | alt & neu, modern
Typ | accommodation: Hotel
Einheiten | units: 40 Zimmer | rooms

Der neu erstellte An- und Umbau des Hotels Hinter-egger liegt in Osttirol im beschaulichen Ort Matrei. Seit Generationen befindet sich das Hotel bereits im Besitz der Familie Hradecky.

Umgeben von wilder Natur steht nun der neueste Umbau modern und selbstbewusst in dem alpinen Ort. Ein alter Kinosaal aus den 30er Jahren ist das Fundament des innovativen Holzbaues. Erbaut wurde er mit Massivholzplatten und verkleidet mit natur-belassenen Lärchenholzbrettern. Die Gestaltung und Raumkomposition ist bewusst einfach gewählt.

Das Ensemble ist nach strengen ökologischen und energiesparenden Maßstäben erstellt worden. Dieses gilt für die Hackschnitzelheizung sowie für die Solar-thermieanlage, die einen Großteil des Warmwasser-bedarfs des Hotels abdecken kann. Für die gestal-terisch-technischen Innovationen gab es eine Reihe von prominenten Auszeichnungen. Für die prämierte Architektur zeichnet das Büro Madritsch-Pfurtscheller, ein auf Holzbau spezialisiertes Architektenduo, verant-wortlich.

Die Zimmer sind reduziert in der Raumform gewählt und mit eigens entworfenem Mobiliar ausgestattet. Schöne, natürliche Materialien ergeben einen erdigen Farbton. Die Übergänge der Materialien sind stufenlos und bilden so einen perfekten Eindruck. Die Zimmer erweitern sich über vorgehängte Loggien nach außen. Ein eigener Wellnessbereich steht den Gästen eben-falls zur Verfügung.

Ein neues, modernes und lichtdurchflutetes Restau-rant ergänzt harmonisch die drei bestehenden Bauernstuben, die gemütliche und traditionelle Gast-freundschaft vermitteln. Der Gastgarten im Schatten des denkmalgeschützten 600 Jahre alten Walter-hauses lädt zum Verweilen ein.

In der Küche legt man großen Wert auf lokale Zutaten und eine kreative Vielfalt in den Küchenkreationen. Insgesamt ist eine schöne neue Interpretation des ländlichen Baustils der Region entstanden.

Matrei liegt im Herzen des Nationalparks Hohe Tauern – Mountainbiken, Wandern, Bergsteigen, Raften, Canycing, Skifahren im Großglockner Resort oder gemütlich relaxen und die Gastfreundschaft der Ost-tiroler genießen – das alles bietet Matrei.

The recently undertaken extension and conversion of Hotel Hinteregger is located in East Tyrol in the tranquil area of Matrei. For generations the hotel has been owned by the Hradecky family.
Surrounded by wild nature, the newest modern conversion stands confidently in its Alpine surroundings. An old cinema hall from the 1930s forms the basis of the innovative wooden construc-tion. It was built with solid wood panels and veneered with natural larch wood boards. The design and room layout is delibe-rately simple. The ensemble was created according to strict ecological and energy-saving principles.
This applies to the wood chip heating and the solar heating system, which covers the majority of the hot water requirements of the hotel. It has won a series of significant awards for its design and technical innovations. The bureau Madritsch-Pfurtscheller, an architectural duo specialised in wooden constructions, is responsible for the award-winning architecture.

The rooms have a minimalistic form and have personally designed furnishings. Beautiful natural materials create earthy colour tones. There are seamless transitions between the different materials, creating an impression of perfection. The rooms are extended towards the exterior with front loggias. The hotel's own wellness area is also available for guests.

A new modern restaurant infused with light rounds off the three existing farmers'parlours harmoniously, offering cosy and traditional hospitality. One is invited to linger in the garden in the shade of the heritage protected 600-year-old Walserhaus.
In the kitchen great emphasis is placed on local ingredients and creative diversity in the cuisine. It is altogether a beautiful new interpretation of the rural building style of the region.

Matrei lies at the heart of the Hohe Tauern National Park- mountain biking, hiking, climbing, rafting, canyoning, skiing in the Großglockner resort or relaxing and enjoying the East Tyrolean hospitality- Matrei offers all of this.

Huberhaus

Schweiz | Switzerland   Bellwald   Oberwallis | Valais

CH-3997 Bellwald
www.magnificasa.ch

Fertigstellung | date of completion: 2008 (Umbau | conversion)
Architekt | architect: Bernhard Stucky, mls-architekten.ch, CH-Zermatt
Architektur | architecture: alt & neu, historisch | alt & neu, historical
Typ | accommodation: Ferienhaus | holiday house
Einheiten | units: 1 Haus | 1 house

Bellwald liegt auf 1.563 m ü. M. auf einer sonnigen Hangschulter mit Aussicht auf das Fieschertal und das Oberwallis. Im Dorfkern bilden die dicht gedrängten Holzbauten schöne Plätze und Gassen. Bellwald ist ein ruhiger Ferienort, der für Sommer- und Winterferien gleichermaßen attraktiv ist. Neben der hervorragenden Lage verfügt das Dorf über ein vielfältiges Sport- und Kulturangebot. In der weiteren Umgebung befinden sich verschiedene Sehenswürdigkeiten, zum Beispiel das Unesco-Weltnaturerbe Aletsch, das Binntal oder das Goms mit seinen traditionellen Dörfern.

Das Huberhaus steht im reizvollen Weiler Eggen, knapp zwei Kilometer vom Hauptdorf entfernt Richtung Fieschertal mit wunderschönem Blick ins Tal. Wenige Wohnhäuser, Spycher und Stadel, gruppieren sich um eine kleine Kapelle aus dem 17. Jahrhundert.
Das Huberhaus ist ein typischer alpiner Holzblockbau aus dem 16. Jahrhundert. Alte Holzbalken, niedrige Decken, eine steile Holztreppe und der Specksteinofen erinnern an das frühere Leben der Bergbauern. Ergänzt mit zeitgenössischen Möbeln und den neuen Küchen- und Sanitäreinrichtungen ergibt sich eine gelungene Mischung aus Alt und Neu. Die Inneneinrichtung, die von der Innenarchitektin Jasmin Grego aus Zürich geplant wurde, besteht aus zeitgenössischen Möbeln von Schweizer Designern und einigen historischen Einrichtungsstücken. Geheizt wird wie früher mit Holz in dem Specksteinofen in der Stube. Im Bad gibt es eine zusätzliche Elektroheizung. Wie früher üblich, sind die Räume niedrig. Die Deckenhöhe in der Stube befindet sich auf nur 1.88 Meter. Das Wohngefühl bleibt so original erhalten. Da sich die Lage zur absoluten Entspannung eignet, wurden auf Fernseher, Telefon- und Internetanschluss verzichtet. Insgesamt bietet das Huberhaus Platz für vier Personen.

Das Haus wird von der gemeinnützigen Stiftung „Ferien im Baudenkmal" betrieben, welche 2005 durch den Schweizer Heimatschutz gegründet wurde. Die Stiftung verbindet Denkmalpflege und Tourismus. Historisch wertvolle Bauzeugen werden übernom-men, sanft renoviert und als Ferienwohnung ver-mietet. Das Modell ermöglicht einen doppelten Gewinn: die Baudenkmäler erhalten eine neue Zukunft, die Feriengäste erleben einen Aufenthalt in einem außergewöhnlichen Gebäude.

Bellwald lies at 1563 metres above sea level on a sunny slope with views over the Fiescher Valley and Oberwallis. The eight wooden buildings crowding the core of the village create pretty squares and alleys. Bellwald is a quiet holiday resort, equally attractive for summer and winter holidays. Apart from the splendid location, the village offers many sports and cultural events. A little further away are various places of interest, such as the UNESCO World Heritage site of Aletsch, the Binn Valley or Goms with its traditional villages.

Huberhaus stands in the charming Weiler Eggen, only about two kilometres from the main village in the direction of the Fiescher Valley, with a wonderful view over the valley. A small number of houses and barns are grouped around a small 17th century chapel. Huberhaus is typical Alpine rustic wooden log cabin from the 16th century. Old wooden beams, low ceilings, steep wooden stairs and a soapstone oven hark back to the former lives of the Alpine farmers. With the addition of contemporary furniture and the new kitchen and bathroom facilities, it successfully blends old and new.
Huberhaus provides accommodation for a total of four people.
The interior design, planned by the interior architect Jasmin Grego from Zürich, consists of contemporary furniture by Swiss designers and also some historical pieces of furniture. The heating, as in the past, is provided by the soapstone oven in the parlour. In addition the bathroom has an electric radiator.
The rooms have low ceilings, as was typical in the past. The ceiling height in the parlour is only 1.88m. This preserves the original living atmosphere.
As the location is conducive to total relaxation there is no TV, telephone or internet.

The house is managed by the charitable fund 'Holidays in heritage buildings', founded by the Swiss Heritage Society. The charity combines heritage protection with tourism. Historically valuable buildings are acquired, carefully renovated and rented out as holiday accommodation. This model has twofold benefits: the heritage sites are assured of a new future and the holiday guests experience staying in an unusual building.

Im Spycher

Schweiz | Switzerland   Fürigen am Bürgenstock   Vierwaldstättersee, Zentralschweiz | Lake Lucerne

Unterschiltstr. 7, CH-6363 Fürigen am Bürgenstock
www.imspycher.ch, info@imspycher.ch
Tel. +41 618 30 66

Fertigstellung | date of completion: 2010 (Umbau | conversion)
Architekt | architect: Thomas Grolimund & Marco Gander
Architektur | architecture: alt & neu, historisch | alt & neu, historical
Typ | accommodation: Ferienhaus | holiday house

Hoch über dem Vierwaldstättersee in Fürigen am Bürgenstock, im Herzen der Schweiz, steht der kleine Spycher wie ein Relikt aus einer längst vergangenen Zeit. Der 300 Jahre alte Spycher wurde vor über 40 Jahren vom Entlebuch nach Fürigen 600 m über dem Meer gebracht. Den Berg Pilatus mit der steilsten Zahnradbahn der Welt im Blickfeld lässt sich der Genius loci (Geist des Ortes) eingebettet in Natur und atemberaubenden Weitblick genießen. Der Standort bietet ein atemberaubendes Panorama über die Berggipfel und den See.

Im Jahr 2010 wurde der kleine Spycher einer sanften Renovation unterzogen. Die neuen Besitzer Tanja Siegwart und Marco Gander achteten vor allem darauf, die grandiose Kulisse in das urige Gebäude zu integrieren und öffneten es zum See hin. Als Kunst- und Architekturliebhaber hat Marco Gander mit seinem Freund, dem Architekten Thomas Grolimund, die Planung gleich selber angefertigt. Die sensible Architektur vereint wie selbstverständlich Behaglichkeit und Design. Individualisten, die sich abseits des Mainstreams bewegen, werden sich hier wohl fühlen. Der kleine Spycher wurde unter ökologischen Gesichtspunkten saniert. Es wurden nur einheimische Hölzer sowie erneuerbare Ressourcen aus der Region verwendet.

Die Küche im Erdgeschoss bietet einen schönen Ausblick während des Kochens. Eine leuchtend olivgrüne Wand wurde mit einer Farbe aus der Farbpalette von Le Corbusier gestrichen. Das darüber liegende Wohnzimmer mit grandiosem Panoramafenster und offener Kaminstelle, welche auch als Ofen genutzt werden kann, bietet eine hervorragende Wohnatmosphäre in Verbindung mit einem wahrhaft beflügelnden Ausblick. Im Außenbereich werden wie selbstverständlich Pantonesessel mit einem IKEA Tisch kombiniert.

Die Schlafzimmer sind mit dem Siebenschläfer des Designers Nils Holger Moormann ausgestattet. Die Einrichtung bildet eine Kombination von alter Holz-decke, weißen Wänden und modernem Mobiliar. Darüber befindet sich das Dachzimmer, ebenfalls als Schlafzimmer nutzbar, als gemütliches „Nest".

Im Vorgarten befindet sich vor der schönen, alten Massivholzeingangstür ein kleiner „Strand" mit zwei Liegestühlen.

High above Lake Lucerne in Fürigen at Bürgenstock, in the heart of Switzerland, stands this small barn like a relic of the distant past. Over 40 years ago the 300-year-old barn was brought to Fürigen from Entlebuch 600 metres across the lake. The genius loci (the protective spirit of the place) embedded in nature enjoys a view of the steepest cog railway in the world on the mountain Pilatus. The location offers a breathtaking panorama of mountain peaks and the lake.

In 2010 the small barn was renovated gently. The new owners Tanja Siegwart and Marco Gander paid special attention to integrating the grand backdrop into the rustic building and opening it up towards the lake. As a lover of art and architecture, Marco Gander carried out the planning himself, together with his friend and architect Thomas Grolimund. The thoughtful architecture naturally blends cosiness and design. Individualists outside of the mainstream will feel comfortable here. The small barn was renovated according to ecological principles. There is exclusive usage of local wood and renewable regional resources.

The kitchen on the ground floor affords a beautiful view whilst cooking. A wall was painted light olive green from the colour palette of Le Corbusier. The living room above with a spectacular panoramic window and an open fireplace, which can also be used as a stove, offers a marvellous living atmosphere in combination with a truly inspirational view. The outside space has Panton chairs combined successfully with an IKEA table.

The bedrooms are furnished with 'Siebenschläfer' ('Dormouse') beds by the designer Nils Holger Moormann. The interior design is a combination of old wooden ceilings, white walls and modern furniture. The attic above can also be used as a bedroom, as a cosy 'nest'.

In front of the beautiful old solid wood entrance door in the front garden there is a small 'beach' with two loungers.

Indulgence Divine

Malta   Birgu

Trip Papa Allessandru VII, MT-1105 Birgu BRG
www.indulgencedivine.com
Tel. +44 781 3988827

Fertigstellung | date of completion: 2010 (Umbau | conversion)
Architekt | architect: Mireille Fsadni, MT-Malta & Gattaldo, UK-London
Architektur | architecture: alt & neu | old & new
Typ | accommodation: Ferienhaus | holiday house

Indulgence Divine versteht sich nicht als Hotel, sondern vielmehr als ein besonderer Urlaubsort für Liebespaare. Dieses originelle Refugium befindet sich in einem Stadthaus aus dem 16. Jahrhundert, unweit des internationalen Yachthafens von Vittoriosa, auf der an Geschichte reichen Insel von Malta. Die Hauptstadt Valletta liegt nur eine kurze Wassertaxifahrt entfernt und die Nähe des übrigen Archipels lädt auch zu großen Entdeckungsfahrten ein.

Das Gebäudeinnere wurde in den letzten Jahren unter der Leitung des in London ansässigen Art Directors Gattaldo restauriert und umgebaut. Der respektvolle Umgang mit dem Bestand durch die Architektin Mireille Fsadni und die geschmackvolle und spielerische Kombination von Designermöbeln und origineller Kunst, Antikmöbeln und Trödel unterstreichen den eleganten Ansatz. Jeder Raum hat eine individuelle Ausprägung und Geschichte. So ist das Schlafzimmer die frühere Hauskapelle, was man noch gut am Kreuzsymbol des Schlusssteines am Steinbogen erkennen kann, sowie auch am Votivgraffiti mit Schiffsmotiven an den Kalksteinwänden.

Das anschließende Badezimmer wird von einer wellenförmigen Doppeldusche geprägt, deren sinnliche Form offen und einladend wirkt. Auch in der Küche wird die Funktionalität durch eine glänzende, schlichte und weiße Küchenzeile auf das Wesentliche reduziert, die einen Kontrast zu den unebenen Wänden bildet, ohne den Raum zu dominieren. Eine Ausnahme stellt der Wohnraum dar. Als eine Art Halbgeschoss ausgeführt, schaffen die weißen Wände und zeitgenössischen Linien eine reizvolle Blickbeziehung mit dem darunter liegenden Essbereich und der höherliegenden Dachterrasse. Eine elegante Wendeltreppe aus Metall verbindet dieses Niveau mit dem Rest der Wohnung.

Einen besonderen Reiz hat die abschließende Dachterrasse. Sie liegt geschützt zwischen massiven Steinwänden und bietet Blicke sowohl auf die engen Altstadtgassen als auch auf den nächtlichen Abendhimmel. Hier kann man den Tag entspannt beginnen und ihn bei einem Glas Wein beenden.

Indulgence Divine is not a hotel. It's a special holiday place to share with a lover. This original retreat is located in a 16th century town house near the international yacht harbour of Vittoriosa, on the historically rich island of Malta. The capital city Valletta is only a water taxi ride away and the short distance to the rest of the archipelago also entices one to embark on great journeys of discovery.

The building's interior was restored and converted in recent years under the direction of the London-based Art Director Gattaldo. The sensitive reconditioning of the fabric of the building by architect Mireille Fsadni and the tasteful and playful combination of bespoke furniture and original art, antique furniture and flea market finds result in a rather elegant solution. Every room has individual characteristics and its own history. The bedroom is the former house chapel, identifiable by the symbol of the crucifix on the archway's keystone and centuries old votive graffiti on its limestone walls featuring ships.

The en-suite features a wave-shaped double shower, its sensuous form open and inviting. In the kitchen the functionality is also reduced to the bare essentials with a glossy ice-white kitchen pod that contrasts with the uneven walls without overpowering the room.
The living room is different. Placed on an intermediate split level, this room with its white walls and contemporary lines creates a charming visual relationship with the dining area below and the roof terrace above. An elegant metal spiral staircase connects this level with the rest of the apartment.

The roof terrace has a particular charm. It lies sheltered between solid stone walls and offers views of the old town's narrow streets as well as the night skies. Here one can start the day in a relaxed fashion and end it with a glass of wine.

Insular Apartments

Deutschland | Germany   Norderney   Ostfriesische Inseln, Nordsee | East Frisian Islands, North Sea

Schulzenstraße 24, D-26548 Norderney
www.insular.de, info@insular.de
Tel. +49 4932 93910, Fax +49 4932 2738

Fertigstellung | date of completion: 2004 (Umbau | conversion)
Architekt | architect: Birgit Stüdemann & Eilt Wessels, D-Norderney
Architektur | architecture: alt & neu | old & new
Typ | accommodation: Apartments
Einheiten | units: 3

Die Insel Norderney ist einer der ostfriesischen Inseln in Niedersachsen, die zwischen der Ems- und Wesermündung liegt. Gute Fährverbindungen gibt es täglich von der Stadt Norddeich. In einer ruhigen, von Bäumen gesäumten Seitenstraße, abseits des touristischen Rummels des Zentrums, liegen die Insular Apartments. Das Haus umfasst drei Apartments eines Bestandsbaus mit Wohnungsgrößen von 45 bis 96 m². Ob für den alljährlichen Familienurlaub mit Freunden oder ein verlängertes Wochenende in entspannter Zweisamkeit, die neu hergerichteten Wohnungen strahlen eine kultivierte und stilistisch besondere Atmosphäre aus, die zum Relaxen einlädt.

"Wohnung 1" verfügt über zwei Schlafräume, ein Bad und ein Wohn- und Eßraum. Viel Licht dringt durch die großen Fenster in den hellen, großzügigen Wohnbereich. Die Holzdeckterrasse mit Garten zum Westen hin lockt bei gutem Wetter zum Verweilen oder Spielen. Bei Schmuddelwetter wird es dank eines offenen Kamins ebenfalls gemütlich.

"Wohnung 2" erstreckt sich über zwei Ebenen. Dort finden sich zwei Schlafräume, ein Bad und ein

geräumiges Eß- und Wohnzimmer. Das alte, offene Gebälk trägt wesentlich zum Charme der Wohnung bei, während mild-cremige, erdige Farben die Wohlfühlatmosphäre unterstreichen die zum abendlichen Glas Wein vor dem Kamin einlädt. Besonderes Highlight dieser Wohnung ist die riesige Terrasse.

Die kleinste Wohnung, Nr. 3, ist ein angebauter Bungalow. Dieser verfügt über einen eigenen Eingang und Terrasse, die vom Wohnzimmeraus erreichbar ist. Ideal für zwei Personen (oder zwei + Kleinkind) muß hier auf nichts verzichtet werden. Die Kochzeile, sowie das Duschbad sind klein aber fein. Eichenparkett liegt zu Füßen und die Einrichtung ist - wie in den anderen Apartments - hell, gemütlich und anspruchsvoll. Eine Sauna im Haupthaus und hauseigenen Fahrräder stehen allen Gästen jederzeit zur Verfügung.

Das Architektenpaar hat weitere Ferienhäuser auf der Nordseeinsel, die ebenfalls in den letzten Jahren saniert wurden. Als „echte" Norderneyer (in der vierten Generation) ist es Ihnen ein Anliegen dem „modernen Wohnen", auf einfühlsam Weise und in Harmonie mit dem Umfeld, Raum auf Ihrer Insel zu geben.

The island of Norderney is one of the East Frisian islands in Lower Saxony, lying between the estuaries of the Ems and the Weser. There are good daily ferry connections from the town of Norddeich. In a quiet tree-lined side road, away from the hustle and bustle of tourism in the old town, lie the Insular Apartments. The original building comprises three apartments ranging from 45 to 96m². Whether for the annual family holiday, with friends or for a long relaxing weekend as a couple, the newly refurbished apartments exude a cultivated and particularly stylish atmosphere conducive to relaxation.

"Apartment 1" comprises two bedrooms, a bathroom and a living and dining area. Lots of light enters through the the large windows into the light and generous living space. The terrace with wooden decking and the west facing garden invites one to relax or play there in good weather. In bad weather it is also cosy owing to the open fireplace.

"Apartment 2" is spread over two floors, with two bedrooms, a bathroom and a spacious dining and living room. The old exposed beams add significantly to the apartment's charm, whilst mild creamy and earthy colours emphasise the atmosphere of well-being, as one enjoys a glass of wine in the evening in front of the fireplace. A particular highlight of this apartment is the vast terrace.

The smallest apartment No. 3 is a bungalow extension. It has its own entrance and a terrace which is accessed from the living room. It is ideal for two people (or two people and a small child) and provides everything one might require. The kitchen unit and the shower room are small but classy. There are oak parquet floors and the interior is – as in the other apartments-light, cosy and sophisticated. A sauna in the main house and its own bicycles are available for guests at any time.

The architectural couple owns other holiday homes on the North Sea island, which have also been renovated in recent years. As 'genuine' Nordeney residents (4th generation) it is important to them to create 'modern living' on their island in an appropriate way and in harmony with the surroundings.

Kavaliershaus

Deutschland | Germany   Fincken   Mecklenburgische Seenplatte | Mecklenburg Lake District

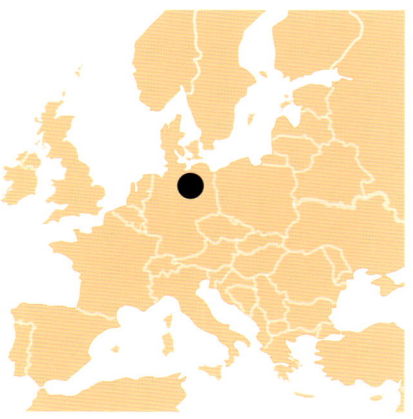

Hofstraße 12, D-17209 Fincken
www.kavaliershaus-finckenersee.de
kavaliershaus@nalbach-architekten.de
Tel. +49 39922 82 700, Fax +49 39922 82 7029

Fertigstellung | date of completion: 2010 (Umbau | conversion)
Architekt | architect: Johanne Nalbach, Lena Nalbach,
                         Nalbach + Nalbach Architekten, D-Berlin
Architektur | architecture: alt & neu | old & new
Typ | accommodation: Zimmer | rooms, Apartments
Einheiten | units: 12 Zimmer | rooms / Apartments

Inmitten der größten Seenlandschaft Deutschlands liegt das Kavaliershaus am Finckener See im Bundesland Mecklenburg-Vorpommern. Das Architektenpaar Johanne und Gernot Nalbach haben zwischen der Müritz und dem Plauener See ihr mittlerweile zweites Hotel eröffnet. Ihr erstes Hotel „Seehotel am Neuklostersee" konnte unter die 100 besten Hotels Europas (Zeitschrift Geo) gewählt werden. Das neue Kavaliershaus zählten die Journalisten des Magazins "GEO Saison" bereits im Eröffnungsjahr zu den "100 besten Hotels unter 100 EUR."

Das klassizistische Kavaliershaus am Finckener See, einst als Teil des Gutes der Familie von Blücher errichtet und zu DDR-Zeiten als Schule genutzt, ist nach einer wechselvollen Geschichte und langen Jahren des Verfalls nun mit großem Aufwand und viel Liebe saniert worden. Es beherbergt zwölf individuell gestaltete Suiten, z.T. mit Kochgelegenheit und Maisonnetten für den Kurz- und Familienurlaub. Für die gesamte Innenarchitektur der Architekten Johanne und Lena Nalbach war die Geschichte des Ortes ein wichtiger Ansatz - ebenso die Werke großer Mecklenburger Künstler und Persönlichkeiten, wie Caspar David Friedrich, Lilienthal, Günther Ücker und Uwe Johnson, die in den Suiten wiederzufinden sind. Die Farb- und Materialwelt ist individuell auf vorhandene konstruktive Elemente bzw. auf das Spiel des natürlichen Lichts in den repräsentativen Räumen abgestimmt. Zu der Hotelanlage mit wunderbarem historischen Baumbestand und eigenem Zugang mit Steg zum Finckener See gehören außerdem ein Frühstücksraum, ein Saunabereich mit Ruheraum und Saunagarten sowie eine kleine Veranstaltungsscheune für Tagungen und Feste. Ausgedehnte Fahrradtouren und Bootsfahrten auf dem See bilden einen Teil der Sportaktivitäten.

Ähnlich dem erfolgreichen Seehotel-Konzept, setzt auch das neue Suitehotel auf die Kraft des Ortes: Fincken - unmittelbar am See gelegen – umgeben von den idyllischen Weiten des Mecklenburger Seenlandes und am Knotenpunkt europäischer Fahrradrouten.

Amidst Germany's largest lakeland area lies Kavaliershaus at Finckener Lake in the federal state of Mecklenburg-Vorpommern. The architect couple Johanne and Gernot Nalbach have opened their second hotel between Müritz and Plauener Lake. Their first hotel 'Seehotel am Neuklostersee' was voted amongst Europe's top 100 hotels (Geo magazine). The new Kavaliershaus was listed by the magazine 'GEO Saison' as one of the "best 100 hotels under 100 EUR".

The classical Kavaliershaus at Finckener Lake, built originally as part of the estate of the Blücher family and used as a school in the former GDR, has now been lovingly and lavishly restored after a chequered history and long years of neglect.
It houses 12 individually designed suites, some of which have kitchen units and maisonettes for short breaks and family holidays. The local history was an important factor in the whole interior design by the architects Johanne and Lena Nalbach, as were the works of great Mecklenburg artists and personalities which adorn the suites, such as Caspar David Friedrich, Lilienthal, Günther Ücker and Uwe Johnson. The colour and material choices are individually adapted to the given construction elements and the

play of natural light in the representative rooms. Apart from the wonderful historic tree population and its own private access to Finckener Lake with a jetty, the hotel also comprises a breakfast room, a sauna area with a relaxation room and a sauna garden, and a small events barn for conferences and parties.

Extensive bicycle tours and boat trips on the lake are amongst the available sporting activities. Following the successful concept of the Seehotel, the new hotel with suites also benefits from the attractiveness of the area: Fincken, right by the lake, surrounded by the idyllic expanse of the Mecklenburg lakeland and at the crossroads of European cycle routes.

La Maison d'Ulysse

Frankreich | France   Baron   Languedoc-Roussillon

Place Ulysse Dumas, FR-30700 Baron - UZES
www.lamaisondulysse.com, contact@lamaisonulysse.com
Tel. +33 4 66 81 38 41, Fax +33 6 48 77 67 70

Fertigstellung | date of completion: 2009 (Umbau | conversion)
Architekt | architect: Frederic Jacquot
Architektur | architecture: modern
Typ | accommodation: Bed & Breakfast, Hotel
Einheiten | units: 5 Zimmer | rooms / Apartments

Mitten in den 'Garrigues', einer Hügellandschaft in den südlichen Cevennen der Provence und dem Languedoc, liegt das Städtchen Baron, überragt von der Burgruine 'Arques'. Hier steht La Maison d'Ulysse, ein charmantes Landhotel.

Das Haus, dessen Ursprünge bis ins 17. Jahrhundert zurückgehen, war Bestandteil einer der alten befestigten Bauernhöfe mit Seidenraupenzucht und Feldern mit Maulbeerbäumen. Zudem ist das Landhaus das Geburtshaus des Dichters und Archäologen Ulysse Dumas (1872-1909), einer Schlüsselfigur der lokalen Geschichte, die der Region wichtige Erkenntnisse über deren vorgeschichtliche Besiedlung brachte.

Guy und Gauthier haben sich des Gebäudes angenommen und es so verwandelt, dass einerseits der ursprüngliche Charakter des Hauses erhalten blieb, es aber andererseits mit modernen Linien, zeitgemäßem Dekor und klaren Eigenschaften begeistert. Umgeben ist das Haus von einem beachtlichen mediterranen Trockengarten, in dem besondere Stauden, Sträucher und Kletterpflanzen wachsen, die dem harschen Klima des Languedoc widerstehen können. Die Terrasse aus Pinienholzbohlen mit angrenzendem Pool verspricht entspannte Stunden. Im schattigen Park laden Maulbeerbäume und uralte Eichen zum Verweilen und Träumen ein. Vollkommene Erholung finden Sie im Hammam, das sich im alten Gewölbe befindet. Die geräumigen Zimmer und Suiten, das Kaminzimmer, der geschützte Innenhof, die gemütliche Bibliothek – das besondere Architekturkonzept der Maison d'Ulysse trägt in großem Maße dazu bei, dass sich die Gäste hier wohl fühlen und ein Gefühl von Ungestörtheit vermittelt bekommen.
In den zwei Zimmern und drei Suiten ist das alte Gebäude besonders gut spürbar, die Einrichtung ist modern bis „stylisch", viele Möbel sind Designerstücke.

In the midst of the 'Garrigues', a hilly landscape in the southern Cévennes of Provence and Languedoc, lies the small town of Baron, dominated by the castle ruins of 'Arques'. The charming country hotel 'La Maison d'Ulysse' is located here.

The house, whose origins go back to the 17th century, was part of one of the old fortressed farmhouses which bred silk worms and had fields with mulberry trees. Furthermore the country house was the birthplace of the poet and archaeologist Ulysse Dumas (1872-1909), a key figure in local history, who made important discoveries about the region's prehistoric settlements.

Guy and Gauthier took on the building and transformed it in such a way that on the one hand the original character of the building was preserved, but on the other hand impressive modern lines, contemporary décor and clear characteristics were added. The house is surrounded by a substantial Mediterranean rockery garden, planted with special shrubs, bushes and climbing plants that can withstand the harsh Languedoc climate. The terrace made of pine wood planks and the adjacent pool provide hours of relaxation. One is invited to linger and dream in the shady park with mulberry trees and ancient oak trees. Complete relaxation is offered by the hammam, located in the old vault. Spacious rooms and suites, the fireplace room, the sheltered interior courtyard and cosy library- these special architectural aspects of the Maison d'Ulysse contribute greatly to the guests' well-being and a feeling of privacy.

In the two rooms and three suites there are traces of the old building. The interior is modern and 'stylish' and a lot of the furniture is designer pieces.

La Romana

Spanien | Spain   La Romana   Alicante, Costa Blanca

CV-840 , ES-03669 La Romana

www.laromanahotel.es, info@laromanahotel.es

Tel. +34 966 192 600

Fertigstellung | date of completion: 2007

Architekt | architect: Isacc Peral, ES-Alicante

Architektur | architecture: alt & neu, modern | old & new, modern

Typ | accommodation: Hotel

Einheiten | units: 18 Zimmer| rooms

Nördlich der mittelspanischen Stadt Alicante liegt das Hotel La Romana. Hier, im Herzen der Provinz Alicante, wurde ein altes Weingut aus dem 19. Jahrhundert zu einer multifunktionalen Hotelanlage umgebaut. Für die Architektur und den Umbau war der bekannte Architekt Isaac Peral verantwortlich. Das schöne, alte Anwesen, das komplett aus lokalem Sandstein erbaut ist, wurde komplett umstrukturiert und mit einigen aufregenden Ausstattungsdetails versehen. So ist neben der modernen Innenausstattung beispielsweise ein abgesenkter „Chill out"-Bereich im Aussenraum entstanden. Hier wird das ruhige und altehrwürdige Bauwerk mit poppig-roten Möbeln geschickt kombiniert. Ein Swimming Pool, eine Bar und diverse Terrassen zum Entspannen umgeben das Anwesen.

Im Innenbereich stehen 18 Zimmer für den Aufenthalt zur Verfügung. Jedes der Zimmer hat einen eigenen Stil. Neben der modernen Einrichtung bietet jedes Zimmer einen hervorragenden Blick auf die Umgebung. Ein Wellnessbereich, der mit hellrotem Naturstein ausgestattet ist und diverse Ruhebereiche beinhaltet, bietet dem gestressten Reisenden eine ruhige und freundliche Atmosphäre.

Das Restaurant, das teilweise mit hellgrünen Sitzmöbelbezügen ausgestattet ist, serviert Kreationen, die durch hohe Qualität, Innovation und Regionalität definiert sind.

Der Aufenthalt kann durch zahlreiche Aktivitäten, wie Reiten, Bergsteigen, Burgbesichtigungen, Golf und anderen Sportarten bereichert werden.

Hotel La Romana lies to the north of the central Spanish town of Alicante. Here, at the heart of the region of Alicante, an old 19th century vineyard was converted into a multifunctional hotel complex. The renowned architect Isaac Peral was responsible for the conversion. The beautiful old building, built entirely of local sandstone, was completely converted and some interesting new features were added. A modern interior design and for example a lower level outdoors 'chill out' area were created, where the calm and time-honoured building is cleverly combined with funky red furniture. A swimming pool, bar and various terraces for relaxation surround the premises.

In the interior 18 rooms are available for guests. Each of the rooms has its own individual style. Apart from the modern furnishing, each room boasts a magnificent view of the surroundings. A wellness area in light red natural stone that comprises various relaxation spaces provides a calm and friendly atmosphere for stressed travellers.
The restaurant, decorated partly with light green seating furniture fabrics, serves high quality and innovative regional creations.

One's stay here can be enhanced with numerous activities such as riding, hiking, castle visits, golf and other sports.

Les Cols Pavellons

Spanien | Spain   Olot   Katalonien | Catalonia

Av. Mas les Cols, ES-17800 Olot

www.lescolspavellons.com

Tel. +34 677 813 817

Fertigstellung | date of completion: 2006

Architekt | architect: RCR Arquitectes, ES-Olot

Architektur | architecture: modern

Typ | accommodation: Hotel

Einheiten | units: 5 Zimmer | rooms

Umgeben von einer einzigartigen Vulkanlandschaft in mitten der katalanischen Pyrenäen liegt oberhalb des Ortes Olot das Hotel & Restaurant Les Cols.
Die Anlage besteht im Kern aus einem alten katalanischen Bauernhof des 13. Jahrhunderts. Dieser wurde zunächst von den katalanischen Architekten Rafael Aranda, Carme Pigem und Ramón Vilalta des Architektur.büros RCR 2002 zum Gourmet-Restaurant „Les Cols" aus- und umgebaut. Auf Wunsch der Betreiber wurde in den Folgejahren im ehemaligen Gemüse-garten des Hofes fünf Gästepavillons hinzugefügt, die das einmalige Erlebnis von Natur, Raum und Architektur vervollständigen.

Die Architekten von RCR verstanden es die örtliche Besonderheit der Vulkanregion mit Wünschen der Betreiber nach einer besonderen Wohnkultur zu verbinden. Die grundlegende Idee war eine komplette Rückführung des Bewohners in ein Gefüge von Harmonie mit der umgebenden Natur.
So besteht das Tragwerk aus feinen Stahlrahmen, die in die transparenten, grün schimmernde Glasplatten

zur Raumausbildung eingesetzt sind. Schichtungen und Überlagerungen mit raumhohen drehbaren Glaslamellen ergeben unterschiedlichste Transparenzen und Farbbrechungen je nach Lichteinfall. Zusätzliche Spiegelungen von Wasserflächen in den Bädern und ein teilweise verglastes Dach erhöhen zudem das Gefühl einer Dematerialisierung der Architektur und einer Aufhebung zwischen Innen- und Außenraum.
Ziel des Projektes ist eine maximale Erholung durch eine Verlangsamung und dem Erleben innerer Ruhe durch die Harmonie mit der natürlichen Umgebung.

Above the town of Olot lies the hotel and restaurant Les Cols, surrounded by a unique volcanic landscape amid the Catalan Pyrenees. The core complex consists of an old 13th century Catalan farmhouse, which was extended and converted in 2002 into the gourmet restaurant 'Les Cols' by the Catalan architects Rafael Aranda, Carme Pigem and Ramón Vilalta from the architectural bureau RCR. At the request of the managers, in the following years five guest pavilions were added in the former vegetable garden in the courtyard, which complete the unique experience of nature, space and architecture.

The RCR architects successfully combined the local characteristics as a volcanic region with the managers' wishes for a special living culture. The basic idea was to immerse the residents completely in the experience of a harmonious merging with the surrounding nature. The rooms are formed by a supporting structure consisting of a slim steel frame into which transparent shimmering green glass panels are set. Different layers with full-length pivotable strips of glass create varying transparencies and colour refractions depending on the incidence of light. Additional reflections from water surfaces in the bathrooms and a partially glazed roof further enhance the feeling of a dematerialisation of the architecture and the blending of the interior with the exterior. The aim of the project is maximum relaxation by slowing down and experiencing inner calm through harmony with the natural surroundings.

Haus Liebing

Deutschland | Germany   Dresden   Sachsen | Saxony

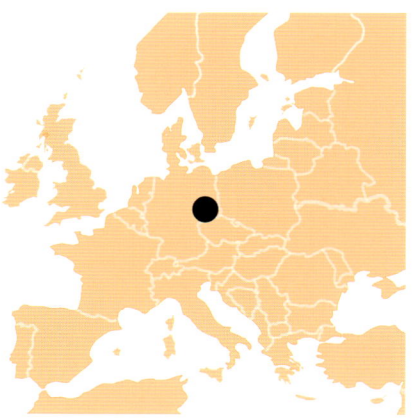

Hoffmannstraße, D-01277 Dresden
www.hausliebing.de

Fertigstellung | date of completion: 2009 (Umbau | conversion)
Architekt | architect: Jens Bauermeister, D-Berlin
Architektur | architecture: alt & neu | old & new
Typ | accommodation: Apartment
Einheiten | unit: 1 Apartment

Die Ferienwohnung im Haus Liebing in Dresden liegt genau in der Mitte zwischen architektonischer Pracht der Altstadt und romantischer Anziehungskraft der sie umgebenden Landschaft: in Blasewitz, dem ältesten Villenviertel Dresdens. Hier ist die großbürgerliche Architektur der Jahrhundertwende in einer Vielfalt wie sonst nirgends erhalten. Zehn Gehminuten vom Blauen Wunder – wie die alte Elbbrücke am Schillerplatz volksmundlich genannt wird – und nur 50 m vom Elbufer entfernt, nimmt die Ferienwohnung das gesamte obere Stockwerk einer denkmalgeschützten Villa aus dem Jahr 1885 ein. Von hier aus lässt sich Dresden und die Umgebung bestens erkunden: Entweder mit dem Rad entlang oder mit dem Schiff auf der Elbe. Die Innenstadt ist einfach mit den öffentlichen Verkehrsmitteln zu erreichen.

Die Wohnung liegt im ersten Geschoss. Von der großzügigen Diele gehen alle Zimmer ab, zur Linken das Wohnzimmer mit seinem Kamin, vor dem man sich auf einer bequeme Sitzgruppe mit zwei Sesseln und einer Couch entspannen kann. Durch eine Doppelflügeltür ist es mit dem Esszimmer verbunden, das mit einem Esstisch mit fünf Stühlen aus Nussholz ausgestattet ist. Am Ende des Flurs befindet sich das geräumige Schlafzimmer. Ein zweites Schlafzimmer befindet sich am anderen Ende des Flurs. Zwei Bäder, mit feiner Keramik ausgestattet, sind zum Teil als en suite angeordnet.
Besonderer Clou: Es gibt kein IKEA Geschirr, sondern edles, englisches Porzellan.

Blickt man auf das gegenüberliegende Elbufer, sieht man die harmonisch in die Landschaft eingebundenen Elbschlösser Schloss Albrechtsberg, Villa Stockhausen und Schloss Eckberg, die Mitte des 19. Jahrhunderts in spätklassizistischem Stil erbaut wurden und von deren Terrassen aus man einen herrlichen Blick über das Elbtal und auf die Stadt hat.

The holiday apartment in Liebing House in Dresden lies exactly halfway between the architectural splendour of the old town and the romantic lure of the surrounding landscape: in Blasewitz, Dresden's oldest villa district. Here the diversity of upper-class turn-of-the-century architecture is preserved better than anywhere else. The holiday apartment is only ten minutes on foot from the Blue Wonder–as the old bridge over the Elbe river at the square Schillerplatz is commonly called- and just 50m from the Elbe embankment. It occupies the whole of the top floor of a heritage-protected villa from 1885. It is a great starting point to discover Dresden and its surroundings, either by bicycle or on a boat along the Elbe. The city centre is easily accessible by public transport from the nearby Schillerplatz.

The apartment is on the first floor. All the rooms lead off the generous hallway. On the left there is the living room with its fireplace, where one can relax on the comfortable suite with two armchairs and a sofa. Double doors open into the dining room, which is furnished with a walnut dining table and five chairs. The spacious master bedroom is at one end of the corridor and a second bedroom at the other end. Two bathrooms, decorated with fine ceramics, are partly en suite.
A wooden veranda with open views extends the apartment towards the exterior.
A notable feature is that there is no crockery from IKEA, but fine English porcelain.

Looking across to the opposite bank of the Elbe one can see the Elbe castles of Schloss Albrechtsberg, Villa Stockhausen an Schloss Eckberg harmoniously nestled into the landscape. They were built in the mid 19th century in the late classical style and their terraces afford glorious views over the Elbe valley and the town.

Manzara

Türkei | Turkey   Istanbul

Galatakulesi Sokak No: 3/2, TR-Kuledibi-Beyoğlu-Istanbul
www.manzara-istanbul.com, info@manzara-istanbul.com
Tel. +90 212 252 4660

Architekt | architect: Erdoğan Altındiş, TR-Istanbul
Architektur | architecture: alt & neu | old & new
Typ | accommodation: Apartments
Einheiten | units: 35 Apartments

Ein wirklich transnationales Konzept hat sich der Architekt und Maler Erdogan Altindis ausgedacht. Besser gesagt: Das Konzept hat sich entwickelt. In der Türkei geboren, wuchs er dennoch in Deutschland auf. Um den perfekten Ort zu finden, musste er den Weg jedoch später in die Türkei zurückfinden. Im Istanbuler Galata-Viertel hat er sich seine erste Wohnung, diese mit einem grandiosen Ausblick, gemietet. Durch die ersten Untervermietungen entstand das Konzept, durch Ferienwohnungen den Austausch der Kulturen erlebbar zu machen. Mittlerweile können eine Reihe von Wohnungen, die sich tief in dem Gewebe der türkischen Metropole befinden und dem Besucher einen Einblick in das wirkliche Leben Istanbuls gewähren, rund um den Galata-Turm gemietet werden. Fast alle Wohnungen haben einen fantastischen Ausblick auf den Bosporus. „Was uns erwartete, kann ich kaum in Worte fassen: Ein Traum aus 1001 Nacht." Diese Beschreibung eines Gastes drückt nur einen Teil der Emotionen aus, die durch die Verbindung der besonderen Unterkünfte mit dem Ort hervorgerufen werden.

Zugleich ist Manzara Istanbul ein Projekt, das Brücken zwischen den Kulturen schlagen und interkulturelle Netzwerke zwischen Ost und West knüpfen soll. Erdogan Altindis entwickelte die Zimmervermittlung zu einer internationalen Begegnungsstätte für Kulturinteressierte . Ihm war es ein Anliegen, durch Kultur als Vermittler zwischen den unterschiedlichen Nationalitäten stehen zu können.

Unter dem Namen „Manzara Perspectives" werden Kunsthappenings seit 2008 abgehalten und erfreuen sich einer regen Anteilnahme. Für die Ausstellungen oder andere Kulturveranstaltungen, wie beispielsweise Lesungen, Vorträge, Filmvorführungen und kleine Konzerte, wo sich lokale und internationale Künstler und Schriftsteller mit interessierten Personenkreisen treffen, verfügt Manzara Perspectives über weitere Räumlichkeiten, etwa in der Suriye Pasajı in der İstiklal Caddesi und Tatar Beyi Sokak.

Darüber hinaus werden Themenführungen angeboten, die eine Gelegenheit bieten, die Stadt mal anders kennen zu lernen.

The architect and painter Erdogan Altindis thought out a truly transnational concept. Or rather: he developed the concept. He grew up in Germany but was born in Turkey. However, to find the perfect location he had to find his way back to Turkey later. In the Galata district of Istanbul he rented his first apartment with a magnificent view. After the first sublettings, the concept evolved of providing the experience of cultural exchange. In the meantime a series of apartments all around the Galata Tower can be rented, located deep within the fabric of the Turkish metropolis and giving the visitor an insight into the real life of Istanbul. Nearly all apartments boast a fantastic view over the Bosporus. 'I can hardly put into words what awaited us, a dream from Arabian Nights.' This description by a guest expresses merely a fraction of the emotions evoked by the combination of the special residences and their location.

At the same time Manzara Istanbul is a project which sets out to build bridges between cultures and establish intercultural connections between east and west. Erdogan Altindis developed the accommodation service into an international meeting place for those interested in culture. He was concerned with being an intermediary between different nationalities through culture.

Art events have been held since 2008 under the name of 'Manzara Perspectives', enjoying lively participation. Manzara Perspectives makes use of further facilities, such as in the streets Suriye Pasaji and Istiklal Caddesi and the gallery in Tatar Beyi Sokak, for the exhibitions and other cultural events such as readings, presentations, film showings and small concerts, where local and international artists and authors meet with interested groups of people.

Furthermore there are themed events offering the opportunity to get to know the town in a different way.

Nebesa

Slowenien | Slowenia Kobarid Oberes Sočatal | Upper Soča valley

Livek 39, SI-5222 Kobarid
www.nebesa.si, info@nebesa.si
Tel. +386 538 44 620

Fertigstellung | date of completion: 2004
Architekt | architect: Rok Klanjšček, Real Engineering d.o.o, SI-Ljublijana
Architektur | architecture: modern
Typ | accommodation: Ferienhäuser | holiday houses
Einheiten | units: 4 Häuser | houses

Hoch über dem Soča-Tal im Westen Sloweniens, direkt an der italienischen Grenze, liegen die vier modern ausgestatteten Cottages in atemberaubender Natur. Bei guter Sicht kann ein herrlicher Ausblick auf die Gebirgszüge des Triglav Nationalparks oder bis ins Friaul genossen werden. Dafür muss aber erstmal auf 900 m Seehöhe gefahren werden. Dann erreicht man die kleine Anlage unterhalb des Berges Kuk, umgeben von einem Rotwildgehege. Hier kann abseits der Hektik des Alltagslebens die Ruhe der nordslowenischen Berge genossen werden.

Die modernen Bauten sind passend zur umgebenden Natur holzverschalt. Im Inneren dominieren klare, ruhige Formen. Das hohe Satteldach erzeugt im Wohnraum eine besondere Stimmung. Man kann es aber auch in der gemütlichen Schlafkammer im ersten Obergschoß geniessen.

Ein Wellness Center mit Swimming Pool, Sauna, Entspannungsraum und einem Jacuzzi bieten neben dem gemeinschaftlichen Kaminzimmer perfekte Relaxatmosphäre. Eine überdachte Terrasse dient als Freisitz, auch wenn das Bergwetter mal schnell umschlagen sollte.

Die Freizeitmöglichkeiten sind unbegrenzt. Neben Bergsteigen, Spazierengehen, Fahrradfahren wird auch Ski fahren und Reiten in nächster Nähe angeboten. Kajak und Kanufahrten gehören genauso zum Sportangebot wie Angeln, Jagen und Paragliding.
In der Umgebung kann durch ausgezeichnete Restaurants die kulinarischen Eigenheiten des Landstrichs erkundet werden. Die Nähe Italiens verleitet zu Besuchen der Stadt Cividale oder eben Udine.

Four cottages with modern furnishings are located in breathtaking nature high above the Soča Valley in western Slovenia, right on the Italian border near the Friulian town of Udine. If one drives up to 900m when there is good visibility one can enjoy magnificent views towards the mountain peaks of Triglav National Park or towards Friuli. Then you reach the small site beneath Kuk mountain, surrounded by a deer-park. Here one can enjoy the peace and quiet of the northern Slovenian mountains, far away from hectic daily life.

The modern buildings are veneered with wood, in accordance with the surrounding nature. The interior is dominated by clear calm forms. The high gabled roof creates a special atmosphere within the living space, which can also be enjoyed in the cosy bedroom on the first floor.

A wellness centre with swimming pool, sauna, leisure room and jacuzzi as well as the communal fireplace room offer the perfect atmosphere for relaxation. A roofed terrace serves as open-air seating, also for those occasions when the mountain weather changes abruptly. The leisure possibilities are unlimited. Apart from mountain climbing, hiking and cycling one can also ski and ride nearby. Kayaking and canoeing are among the sport options, along with fishing, hunting and paragliding.

One can sample the culinary specialities of the region in many excellent local restaurants. The proximity of Italy invites one to visit towns such as Cividale or Udine.

Nordic
Watercolour

Schweden | Sweden   Skärhamn   Västergötland

SE-47132 Skärhamn
www.akvarellmuseet.se
Tel. +46 304 60 00 80

Fertigstellung | date of completion: 2000
Architekt | architect: Niels Bruun & Henrik Corfitsen, DK-Vanløse
Architektur | architecture: modern
Typ | accommodation: Ferienhäuser | holiday houses
Einheiten | units: 5 Häuser | houses

Auf der westschwedischen Insel Tjörn befindet sich das Nordische Aqurellmuseum. Die Insel liegt unweit von Göteborg und ist einfach erreichbar. In den Sommermonaten verdoppelt sich die Einwohnerzahl des Örtchens Skärhamn durch die Anzahl der Touristen. Die Gegend ist bekannt für die Schärenlandschaft mit ihren schroffen Felsufern und beliebt bei Seglern und Kajakfahrern, Skärhamn hat eine bekannt Marina.

Das Nordische Aqurellmuseum in der Stadt ist eines der bedeutensten Kulturprojekte an der schwedischen Westküste und zieht inzwischen viele Besucher an. Das Museum versteht sich auch als Zentrum für zeitgenössische Kultur im Bereich Forschung und Ausbildung der Aquarellmalerei. Hier können Kurse im Aqurellmalen belegt oder die wechselnden Ausstellungen besucht werden. Ein Restaurant mit großer Aussenterrasse komplettiert das Ensemble, das als moderne Form 1996 entworfen wurde. Sieger des Architekturwettbewerbes war damals das Büro der dänischen Architekten Niels Bruun & Henrik Corfitsen. Aktuell gibt es Planungen für die Erweiterung des Museums.

Der hellrote Farbton des Museumsgebäudes entspricht der klassischen schwedischen Farbe aber auch der Farbgebung bekannter Aquarellgemälde. Auf der nur wenige Meter entfernten gegenüber befindlichen Küste wurden als Künstlerateliers fünf kubische Einzelbauten errichtet. Sie schweben mit Teilen des Körpers leicht über dem Wasser und treten so in einen visuellen Kontakt mit dem Museum. Die Ateliers sind Einzimmerapartments mit Empore und Blick auf das Aquarellmuseum. Sie werden auch an Besucher und Urlauber vermietet.

The Nordic Watercolour Museum is located on the western Swedish island of Tjörn. The island isn't far from Göteborg and is easily accessible. In the summer months the population of the little town of Skärhamn doubles with the influx of tourists.
The area is renowned for its skerry landscape with its rugged cliff shores and it is popular with sailors and kayakers. Skärhamn has a famous marina.

The Nordic Watercolour Museum in the town is one of the most significant cultural projects on the west coast of Sweden and now attracts many visitors. The museum also acts as a centre of contemporary culture as regards research and training in watercolour painting. One can attend watercolour painting courses or varying exhibitions. A restaurant with a large exterior terrace completes the ensemble, which was designed in 1996 in a modern formation. At the time the Danish architect bureau Niels Bruun & Henrik Corfitsen won the architectural competition. There are current plans to extend the museum.

The light red colour scheme of the museum building corresponds to the classic Swedish colour but also the colour scheme of famous watercolour paintings. On the opposite shore just a short distance away five cubed individual buildings were built as artists' ateliers. Parts of them float just above the water, thereby making visual contact with the museum.
The ateliers are single room apartments with rood lofts and views of the watercolour museum. They are also rented out to visitors and holiday makers.

Refugio Son Pons

Spanien | Spain   Campanet-Ullaró   Mallorca

ES-07310 Campanet-Ullaró
www.refugiosonpons.com, info@refugiosonpons.de
Tel. +34 971 516837

Fertigstellung | date of completion: 1999
Architekt | architect: Manfred Tumfart, D-Kaarst
Architektur | architecture: alt & neu | old & new
Typ | accommodation: Hotel
Einheiten | units: 6 Zimmer | rooms

Auf der Insel Mallorca liegt die Finca Refugio Son Pons. Das Hotel befindet sich im Nordosten der Insel, ruhig und abgeschieden von jeglichem Tourismus und ist dennoch schnell von Palma aus erreichbar. Die traumhafte nähere Umgebung lädt zu Bergwanderungen, ebenso wie Strandbesuchen ein.

Das Haus ist im 13. Jahrhundert erbaut worden und besteht aus dem Herrenhaus und seinen vielfältigen Anbauten zur ehemaligen Bewirtschaftung des Landguthofs. Liebevoll restauriert und mit außergewöhnlichen Details versehen, umschließen die Zimmer den zentralen, romantischen Innenhof mit seinem original mittelalterlichen Brunnen. Die Mauern von Son Pons wurden vor mehr als siebenhundert Jahren aus dem umliegenden Felsgestein errichtet. Heute zeugen die zum Teil naturbelassenen Steinflächen von den Geschichten der Belagerer und Herrscher, dem einfachen Landleben und der Geschichte der adeligen Familie Pons, die das Anwesen begründete.
Jeder Raum des Anwesens, seine Funktion und Geschichte, wurde vom Architekten Manfred Tumfart eingehend untersucht. In liebevoller Kleinarbeit wurden Details herausgearbeitet, spannungsvolle Kontraste geschaffen und Räume durch geschickte Lichtführung erweitert. Der von ihm geschaffene ästhetische Rahmen erhält die Grundqualitäten des Bauwerks und erschafft zugleich, auch durch die Integration von Skulpturen und Fundstücken, einen

individuellen Ausdruck. Der Umbau wurde 1999 abgeschlossen.

Sechs Zimmer befinden sich im altehrwürdigen Anwesen. Diese sind individuell modern reduziert gestaltet, ohne den Charme des alten Gemäuers in Frage zu stellen. Die Zimmer haben unterschiedliche Größen bis zur Suite Principal mit 55 m² Wohnfläche. Das Haus hält eine Reihe von Zusatzangeboten, wie Yoga, Weinproben oder Massagen bereit.
In nur zwei Minuten Entfernung befindet sich das „Zentrum für Naturschutz im Mittelmeerraum". Dieses veranstaltet deutschsprachige Wanderungen während der die Besonderheiten der einheimischen Natur erklärt werden.

The finca Refugio Son Pons is on the island of Mallorca. The hotel is located in the north east of the island, in a quiet and remote spot away from all tourism, but nevertheless easily accessible from Palma. The magnificent immediate surroundings offer hiking and visits to the beach.

The house was built in the 13th century and consists of a manor house and its many extensions for servicing the country estate. The rooms were lovingly restored, with the addition of unusual details, and they surround the romantic central interior courtyard with its original medieval fountain. The walls of Son Pons were built more than seven hundred years ago with the local craggy rocks. Today the partly natural stone surfaces bear witness to the stories of the besiegers and rulers, the simple rural life and the history of the noble Pons family who founded the estate.
Every room of the estate, its function and its history, was researched extensively by the architect Manfred Tumfart. Details were uncovered painstakingly,

interesting contrasts were created and rooms extended by the clever channelling of light. His aesthetic framework forms the basic standard of the building and creates and individual impression through the integration of sculptures and interesting finds. The conversion was completed in 1999.

The time-honoured estate comprises six rooms. These are designed in an individual, modern and minimalistic style, without overshadowing the charm of the old walls. The rooms are of different sizes, the largest being the 55m² Suite Principal.
The house offers a series of additional leisure activities, such as yoga, wine tasting or massages. Just two minutes away is the 'Mediterranean Centre for Nature Protection', organising German language walks presenting the peculiarities of the local nature.

Salvinia Lodge

Polen | Poland   Stegna   Ostsee | Baltic Sea

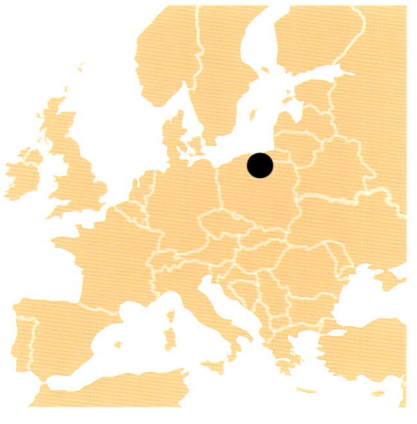

Przemyslaw 4, PL-82103 Stegna
www.salvinialodge.pl, m.karwacka@salvinialodge.pl
Tel. +48 692 496 619

Fertigstellung | date of completion: 2006 (Umbau | conversion)
Architekt | architect: J. Schülke, D-Berlin; M. Adamus, PL-Sopot
Architektur | architecture: alt & neu, historisch | old & new, historical
Typ | accommodation: Ferienhaus | holiday house
Einheiten | units: 3 apartments

Nur etwa 35 km von Danzig entfernt liegt die Region Żuławy im Mündungsdelta der Weichsel (früher Marienwerder genannt). Eine Landschaft mit Weiden und Pappeln, verschlafenen kleinen Dörfern und gesundem Ostseeklima. Alte Linden, Kastanien und Eichen säumen endlose Alleen, Feldreine, Bauernhöfe und Kirchen. Unzählige Wasserstrassen und Kanäle schlängeln sich durch die Landschaft.
In Strandnähe liegt der denkmalgeschützte Holz- und Fachwerkhof Salvinia Lodge. Das Haus wurde bereits 1789 erbaut. Der Altbau wurde 2005/2006 über zwei Jahre von Grund auf restauriert und mit viel Liebe zum Detail modern erweitert.

Das Haus ist eines der wenigen noch erhaltenen Vorlaubenhäuser protestantischer Siedler und daher eine der Touristenattraktionen zwischen Danzig und Elblag. Hier wohnten vor 200 Jahren Mennoniten, die aus der Täuferbewegung der Schweiz entstanden sind und ehrbare Prinzipien wie Ablehnung des Eides und des Militärdienstes verfolgten. Es ist das einzige Haus seiner Art in der gesamten Region, das als Gästehaus genutzt wird.

Das Haus ist ein Holzbau. Die Wände sind zum Teil lehmverputzt und verströmen in Verbindung mit dem wohltuenden Ostseeklima eine entspannende Atmosphäre.
Bei der Sanierung wurde Wert auf die Erhaltung der Alterungsspuren der Oberflächen gelegt. Diese wurden mit neuen Materialien kombiniert, so dass eine einzigartige Ausstrahlung von neuen und alten Oberflächen und Elementen entstanden ist.

Am Umbau haben zwei Architekten mitgewirkt: Jürgen Schülke aus Berlin und die polnische Innenarchitektin Magdalena Adamus vom Büro Loft.

Es stehen neben den großzügigen Allgemeinbereichen Küche, Speisezimmer und Diele drei Apartments mit Schlaf-, Wohn- und Badezimmer zur Verfügung. Die historische „gute Stube" konnte weitestgehend in ihrem Ursprungszustand erhalten werden und ist Bestandteil des Apartments im Erdgeschoss. Im Grünen Zimmer im ersten Obergeschoss in der alten Kornkammer wurde eine antike Hoftür aus Indien integriert. Im „Comix-Zimmer" überrascht neben der fast 6m hohen Raumhöhe eine Badezimmergestaltung mit Jules Vernes Geschichte von Käpt´n Nemo. Alle Zimmer sind elegant und modern mit ausgesuchten Designermöbeln eingerichtet. In den Bädern überraschen liebevoll ausgesuchte Details.

In der Region lassen sich neben Besuchen des Weltkulturerbes in Danzig, Marienburg oder Frauenburg ausgiebige Strandspaziergänge, erholsame Radtouren in der flachen Landschaft des Flussdeltas, Fahrten mit einer historischen Schmalspurbahn oder Reitausflüge am Strand und den ausgedehnten Kiefernwäldern machen. Ein Highlight ist eine Tour mit selbstgesteuerten Motorbooten auf den alten Weichselarmen bis ins Frische Haff.

Only about 35km from Danzig lies the region of Żuławy in the estuarial delta of the Weichsel river (formerly called Marienwerder). It is a landscape of meadows, poplars and sleepy little villages, with a healthy Baltic Sea climate. Old linden, chestnut and oak trees line endless avenues, field borders, farm houses and churches. Countless waterways and canals meander through the landscape.

Near the beach lies Salvinia Lodge, a heritage protected wood and half-timber building. The house was built as early as 1789. Over the course of two years in 2005/2006 the original building was restored completely and extended in a modern style with careful attention to detail.

The house is one of the few still remaining houses with a front gable built by Protestant settlers and is therefore one of the tourist attractions between Gdansk and Elblag. 200 years ago Mennonites lived here, who evolved from the Anabaptist movement in Switzerland and followed worthy principles like the rejection of oaths and of military service. It is the only house of its kind in the whole region which is used as a guest house.

The house has a wooden construction. The walls have partial loam rendering and exude a relaxing atmosphere, as does the refreshing Baltic Sea climate. During the renovation care was taken to preserve the signs of ageing on the surfaces. These were combined with new materials, creating a unique vibe of new and old surfaces and elements.
Two architects contributed to the conversion: Jürgen Schülke from Berlin and the Polish interior architect Magdalena Adamus from Büro Loft.

Apart from the generous communal areas with kitchen, dining room and hallway there are three apartments available with a bedroom, living room and bathroom. The historical parlour was largely preserved in its original state and forms part of the ground floor apartment. An antique courtyard gate from India was integrated into the Green Room on the first floor in the former granary. The 'Comix Room' has the surprising features of a ceiling height of nearly 6m and a bathroom design with the Jules Vernes story of Captain Nemo. All rooms are elegant and modern with select designer furniture. The bathrooms feature carefully chosen details.

Apart from visits to World Heritage cultural sites in Gdansk, Marienburg or Frauenburg, the region offers lengthy strolls along the beach, relaxing cycle tours in the flat landscape of the river delta, rides on a historic narrow-gauge railway or horse riding excursions to the beach and the extensive pine forests. One of the highlights is a tour with self-driven motorboats on the old channels of the Weichsel to the Vistula Lagoon.

Essay **Erich Prödl**

Die Wiederentdeckung des Bekannten

Das private Haus sagt viel über die Persönlichkeit und Haltung seines Erbauers aus. Insbesondere in einer Zeit, in der der private Repräsentationsdruck stetig wächst, ist die zweite Moderne teilweise zu einem engen, fast ideologischen Manifest der Errungenschaften des Selbst degradiert worden. Der Wiener Architekt und spätere Exilant im sicheren Schweden der Kriegsjahre, Josef Frank, sagte einmal: "Der Mensch lässt sich lieber einen Raubmord vorwerfen als schlechten Geschmack."

Das Haus als Ausdruck des Selbst muss sitzen wie ein maßgeschneiderter Anzug. Es ist ein Manifestiert des Ich und positioniert es in der Gesellschaft. Das individuelle Haus kontrolliert die Riten des Alltags im überblendeten Maß.

Schon in den Gründungsjahren der Moderne nahmen die Architekturströmungen sichtbare Zeichen einer radikalen Definition des Wohnens an. So artikulierte der Amerikaner Frank Lloyd Wright den amerikanischen Traum durch das intensive Zusammenspiel zwischen Innen- und Außenraum. Der Österreicher Adolf Loos drückte urbane Verdichtungen durch komplexe innenräumliche Strukturen, den Raumplan, aus. Die Ikone der frühen Moderne, Le Corbusier, definierte das Wohnhaus gar als funktionale Maschine.

Ich denke, dass ein leichtes Unbehagen der selbstauferlegten Kontrolle im modernen Wohnkonzept mitschwingt. Aber was ist im Laufe der Zeit verloren gegangen? Wo ist die Leichtigkeit, die sinnliche Erfahrungsfreude und das subjektiv gefühlte Mystische des Hauses aus der Kindheit geblieben?

Auf diese Frage gibt es sicherlich Hunderte von Antworten. Eine Art der Wiederentdeckung lässt das Ferienhaus zu. Das enge Korsett des Alltags, geschnürt durch die hundert Sachzwänge des Alltagslebens, weicht dem leichten und freien Sommerhemd. Die kurze Hose inspiriert zum Entdecken und das Sommerkleid zum unbeschwerten Sein. Diese vielleicht fremden Kleidungsstücke eröffnen die Möglichkeit, Kindern gleich spielerisch in eine andere, aber nicht fremde Form des Seins zu schlüpfen. Das Ferienhaus lädt ein, Gewohntes zu hinterfragen und neue Seiten und Bedürfnisse zu entdecken. Gleichzeitig ist das neue Umfeld ein schöner Weg zurück in die Erfahrungen unserer Kindheit: Barfuss zu gehen und die Steine unter den Füßen zu spüren, den Stall und seine Gerüche wiederzuentdecken, das warme Holz an

seinem Rücken zu spüren und nachts das Knarren der Holzstiege ängstlich und neugierig zugleich wahrzunehmen. Morgens ist das Bad an ungewohnter Stelle, das Buch wird nachmittags bei neuem und unbekanntem Kaffeegeruch in der Küche gelesen und die Kinder werden in knarzenden Bauernbetten zum Schlafen gelegt.

Ich teile mit dem großem italienischen Architekten Aldo Rossi die Meinung, dass wir auf der Suche nach „etwas" nicht nur dieses „etwas" suchen. Die Suche allein lässt uns vieles wiederentdecken, das lange als verschüttet und verloren galt. Noch drastischer hat Thomas Bernhard, der sich zum Schreiben immer wieder in seinen alten, umgebauten Bauernhof zurückzog, seine Erfahrungen 1964 beschrieben. „Ich höre, was ich noch nie gehört habe, ich sehe, was ich noch nie gesehen habe, ich denke, was ich noch nie gedacht habe, ich fühle, was ich noch nie gefühlt habe".

Es gibt, behaupte ich, zwei überaus lohnende Gründe, das Zuhause zu verlassen und uns, wenn auch nur für eine kurze Zeit, an fremde Orte zu begeben: Die Suche nach dem Neuen, Unbekannten und die Wiederentdeckung von Bekanntem und bereits Verlorengegangenem.

Diese Suche bedeutet aber auch, bewusst nach außen zu gehen und sich auszusetzen, während das Wiederentdecken eher einer Reise ins eigene Innere gleicht.

Das Ferienhaus ist das Gegenteil vom Pauschalurlaub und ermuntert diese Suche. Es ermutigt zum Beispiel zum Entdecken des örtlichen Marktes und fordert zum aktiven Teilnehmen am öffentlichen Leben auf. Die täglichen Wege wollen gefunden und die Umgebung will erkundschaftet werden.

Ein eigener Tagesablauf muss auf schnelle Art und Weise in das temporäre Heim installiert werden. Zu den rationalen Einteilungen des Tages gesellt sich geschwistergleich die Erkundung des Neuen durch die Sinne.

Und warum soll diese wunderbare Form der neuen Entdeckungen eines Ortes und seines Selbst nicht in faszinierender und außergewöhnlicher Architektur stattfinden?

Erich Prödl
Architekt und Städteplaner

Geboren 1964 in Graz
Architekturstudium an der Akademie der bildenden Künste in Wien
Städtebaustudium an der Columbia University in New York, USA
Architekturbüro in Graz
Lehrtätigkeit an amerikanischen und österreichischen Universitäten
Professur für Bauen im Kontext an der Hochschule Regensburg

The rediscovery of the familiar

Private houses reveal a lot about the personality and attitude of their builders. Especially at a time when the pressure to represent one's private self is steadily increasing, the second wave of modernity has been partly reduced to a narrow, almost ideological manifestation of the achievements of the self. The Viennese architect Josef Frank, later an expatriate in the safe Sweden of the war years, once said: 'People would rather be accused of a holdup murder than of bad taste.'

The house as an expression of the self must fit like a tailored suit. It is a manifestation of the ego and positions it in society. The individual house controls the rituals of daily life to a large degree.

Already in the founding years of the modern era architectural trends adopted visible signs of a radical definition of living. And so the American Frank Lloyd Wright articulated the American dream through the intensive interplay between interior and exterior spaces. The Austrian Adolf Loos expresses urban agglomerations by means of complex interior space structures and layouts. The icon of the early modern era, Le Corbusier, even defined the residential house as a functional machine.

I think that a certain unease accompanies the self-imposed control in the modern living concept. But what has been lost over the course of time? What happened to the lightheartedness, the sensual joy of experience and the subjectively felt mystic aspect of one's childhood home?

There are surely hundreds of answers to this question. The holiday home enables a form of rediscovery. The light and free summer shirt is freed from the narrow corset of daily life, tied with hundreds of daily obligations. Shorts inspire discovery and summer dresses encourage being carefree. These perhaps unfamiliar items of clothing open up the possibility for children to slip playfully into a different but not unknown state of being. The holiday home invites the questioning of the habitual and the discovery of new perspectives and needs. At the same time the new environment is a beautiful way back into the experiences of childhood: to walk barefoot and feel the pebbles under our feet, to rediscover stables and their smells, to feel the warm wood behind one's back and to perceive the creaking of the wooden steps at night with both fear and curiosity. In the morning the bathroom is in a different place, in the afternoon one reads books in the kitchen accompanied by the new and unfamiliar aroma of coffee, and the children are put to bed in creaking farmer beds.

I share the opinion of the great Italian architect Aldo Rossi, that in the search for 'something' we are not looking only for this 'something'. The search itself enables us to discover many things anew that for a long time had been considered buried and lost. Thomas Bernhard, who withdrew repeatedly to his old converted farmhouse to write, described his experiences even more radically in 1964:
'I hear what I've never heard before, I see what I've never seen before, I think what I've never thought before, I feel what I've never heard before.'

I believe there are definitely two worthwhile reasons to leave our home and to make our way to a foreign place, even if only for a short time: the search for what is new and unknown, and the rediscovery of what is known and already lost.

This search also entails, however, to leave and consciously expose oneself to something new, whilst rediscovery is more like a journey into one's own self.

The holiday home is the opposite of a package holiday and stimulates this search. It encourages for example the discovery of the local market and active participation in public life. The daily paths want to be found and the surroundings want to be explored. A daily plan has to be installed quickly in the temporary home. Apart from rationally dividing up the day, the discovery of the new awakens the senses.

And why should this wonderful form of new discovery of a place and of oneself not take place within fascinating and unusual architecture?

Erich Prödl
Architect and urban planner

Born 1964 in Graz
Architecture studies at the Academy of Fine Arts in Vienna
Urban planning studies at Colombia University in New York, USA
Architecture bureau in Graz
Teaching positions at American and Austrian universities
Professorship for construction at Regensburg University

Spielberg5

Deutschland | Germany   Freiamt-Reichenbach   Schwarzwald | Black Forest

Am Spielberg 5, D-79348 Freiamt-Reichenbach
www.spielberg5.de, haus@spielberg5.de

Fertigstellung | date of completion: 2010 (Umbau | conversion)
Architekt | architect: Peter Dallmann, D-Freiburg
Architektur | architecture: modern
Typ | accommodation: Ferienhaus | holiday house
Einheiten | units: 1 Haus | 1 house

Mitten in den waldigen Bergen des Schwarzwaldes erreicht man nach romantischer Anfahrt das Ferienhaus Spielberg5.

Malerisch liegt es oberhalb der Gemeinde Freiamt-Reichenbach und war bis vor kurzem ein noch wenig beachtetes Bauernhaus. Doch das Potenzial, das die Verbindung traditioneller Architektur mit zeitgenössischem Design und moderner Technik entwickeln kann, wurde 2009/2010 mit viel Engagement und Liebe zum Detail erkannt und erfolgreich entwickelt. Auf den ersten Blick erscheint das in Gelb gehaltene Gebäude vertraut und zurückhaltend. Doch sobald man das Innere betritt, wird sofort die Einzigartigkeit dieses Projektes klar. Gläserne Schiebetüren, freigelegte Holzkonstruktionen und Steinwände geben den Wohn- und Gemeinschaftsräumen einen sehr individuellen Charakter, der durch den gezielten Einbau moderner Funktionselemente, wie der Kochzeile mit ihrer Sitzgelegenheit oder dem Kamin mit integrierter beheizter Sitznische, bewusst kontrastiert wird. Über drei Geschosse verteilt verfügt das Haus über insgesamt drei Schlafzimmer mit Doppelbetten, ein Studio im Dachgeschoss sowie eine gut eingerichtete Wohnküche und einen gemütlichen Salon mit offenem Kamin mit einer Kapazität für ca. acht Personen. Alle Schlafzimmer atmen den Charme des alten Bauernhauses mit ihren sorgsam ausgewählten Holzböden und einer insgesamt wohltuend zurückhaltenden Ausstattung.
Die Bäder verfügen über ebenerdige Duschen und teilweise sogar über eine eigene Badewanne.

Besonderes Highlight ist der Wellnessbereich mit Sauna und Liegen zum Entspannen sowie ein großes Sonnendeck auf der Dachebene. Von dort genießt man einen eindrucksvollen Panoramablick auf die umliegenden Berge des Schwarzwaldes. Besondere Erwähnung soll an dieser Stelle noch die originelle Treppe im Inneren finden. Sie wurde als elegant geschwungene, hölzerne Sambatreppe ausgebildet.

Right in the middle of the forested hills of the Black Forest lies the holiday home Spielberg5. A romantic approach leads to it. It lies picturesquely above the municipality of Freiamt-Reichenbach and until recently it was a farm house that was easily passed by. However, its potential to combine traditional architecture with contemporary design and modern technology was recognised and successfully realised in 2009/2010 with a great deal of dedication and attention to detail. At first glance the yellow building appears familiar and modest. However, as soon as one steps into the interior the uniqueness of the project becomes clear. Glass sliding doors, exposed wooden beams and stone walls lend the living and communal rooms a very individual character. This is contrasted deliberately with the purposeful integration of modern functional elements, such as the kitchen unit with its seating or the fireplace with an integrated heated sitting nook. Spread over three floors, the house can accommodate about eight people and comprises a total of three bedrooms with double beds, a studio in the attic, a well-equipped kitchen diner and a cosy lounge with an open fireplace. All bedrooms exude the charm of an old farm house with their carefully chosen wooden floors and generally soothing conservative furnishings.

The bathrooms have walk-in showers and some even have their own bathtub.
The wellness area is a special highlight, with a sauna and loungers for relaxing and a large sun terrace on the roof. From there you can enjoy an impressive panoramic view of the surrounding hills of the Black Forest.
The original interior stairs are also very noteworthy, with the form of elegantly curved, wooden samba stairs.

Skinidin - Black Shed

Großbritannien | Great Britain   Skinidin   Schottland, Insel Skye | Scotland, Isle of Skye

2 Skinidin, Isle of Skye, UK-Iv55 8ZS
www.blackshed.co.uk, hello@blackshed.co.uk
Tel. +44 01470 521214

Fertigstellung | date of completion: 2008
Architekt | architect: Rural Design, UK-Dunvegan
Architektur | architecture: modern
Typ | accommodation: Ferienhaus | holiday house
Einheiten | units: 1 Haus | 1 house

Das Architekturbüro Rural Design ist spezialisiert auf kleine Bauten, die sich in die Landschaft und Kultur Schottlands einfügt. Eine Reihe wohldesignter Bauten ist entstanden die bereits mehrfach preisgekrönt wurden.

Das Projekt wird von den Planern selbst betrieben. Es liegt mit einmaliger Aussicht auf der vor Schottland gelegenen Insel Skye und wurden 2009 quasi als die Urhütte des Gasthauses im ländlichen Umfeld ausgedacht.

Das kleine, in schwarzem Farbton gehaltene Bauwerk soll bewusst die Beziehung zu den umliegenden alten Bauernhäuser herstellen. Das normale Image des weißen Kubusbauwerks als schönes Fotoimage soll hier umgangen werden und die alte Tradition benutzter Bauten aufgenommen werden. Das 70 m² große Gebäude ist eingeschossig und umfasst eine Lounge/Wohnbereich, ein Schlafzimmer, ein Badezimmer und ein study space. Die einfache Holzlattung der Aussenfassade und die direkt sichtbaren Verbindungen verbreiten eine Atmosphäre der originalen Wildheit der schottischen Umgebung. Beheizt wird das ganze durch einen Holzofen. Eine Besonderheit kann aber nicht gesehen werden: Die Dämmung ist aus Schafswolle und erzeugt ein hervorragendes Raumklima. Die einfachen großen Fenster rahmen die Landschaft. Einen 270 Grad Ausblick hat man durch die „ausgebissene" Ecke, die gleichzeitig Eingang und Terrasse markiert.

Innen sind die Räume in einfacher Holzverschalung gehalten. Der Fussboden ist als geschliffener Estrich ausgeführt worden.

Auf eine besondere Beziehung zur Umwelt wurde nicht nur für die Dämmung Wert gelegt. Die Betten sind aus organischen Baumwolle hergestellt.

Das Wasser kommt aus dem eigenen Brunnen. Das Wasser wird regelmäßig getestet. Auf Anfrage kann selbstgebackenes Brot, frische Eier und Gemüse aus dem eigenen Garten geliefert werden.

Das Haus wurde nicht nur als Gasthaus für den einen Zweck konzipiert, sondern soll auch als Prototyp für kostengünstiges Wohnen in ganz Schottland als Beispiel dienen.

The award winning architectural practice Rural Design based on the Isle of Skye specialises in buildings which blend into Scotland's landscape and culture. The Black Shed is one of them and it is perfectly situated at the foot of the Macleod's Table mountain with a unique view towards the Western Isles which lie off the Scottish coast.

The small black building consciously seeks a connection to the surrounding old croft houses. The typical image of a classic white croft house was avoided in favour of adopting the vernacular of traditional farm buildings.

The 70m² building is on one level and comprises a lounge/living area, bedroom, bathroom and study space. The simple timber cladding on the external façade and the profile roof sheeting connect back into the landscape, blending into the wilderness of its Scottish hillside surroundings.

The building is heated throughout with under floor heating and is complemented with a wood-burning stove, which combined with the sheep's wool insulation creates an excellent indoor climate. Large landscape windows help to frame the surrounding countryside and a 270º view is afforded by the 'bitten off' corner, which also marks the porch entrance and the deck. Large external sliding doors provide protection from storms in the winter and shade for the Highland summer sun. The interior walls throughout the building are clad in timber and the floor is polished concrete.

When clients arrive for their holiday they are welcomed with homemade bread, scones and fresh eggs from the croft. The large king size bed is made up with organic cotton bedlinen and there are sumptuous linen bath towels. The water is sourced from a spring on the hill.

The house was not conceived just for the purpose of holiday accommodation, but it is also intended to serve as an example of a Scottish prototype of economical living.

Strandhaus Böhl

Deutschland | Germany   St. Peter-Ording   Nordsee | North Sea

Böhler Landstraße 175a, D-25826 St. Peter-Ording
www.strandhausboehl.de, kontakt@strandhausboehl.de
Tel. +49 172 436 12 03

Fertigstellung | date of completion: 2010
Architekt | architect: 360grad+ architekten, D-Hamburg
Architektur | architecture: modern
Typ | accommodation: Ferienhaus | holiday house
Einheiten | units: 2 Häuser | 2 houses

Zwei strahlend weiße Baukörper stehen mit Blick auf die Nordsee am Strand von St. Peter-Ording. Bei warmem Wetter hält diese nordisch-maritime Lage jedem Vergleich in Hinsicht auf Urlaubsqualität und Atmosphäre mit dem Mittelmeer stand.

Die Halbinsel um St. Peter-Ording bietet hervorragende Strand- und Meeresurlaubsmöglichkeiten. Weite Strände, grüne Wiesen und versteckte Buchten bilden den Hintergrund für die elegante Konstruktion der Strandhäuser Böhl. Das Grundstück mit über 900 m² liegt direkt hinter einer Naturdüne und ist in ein Ferienhausgebiet eingebunden. Schleswig-Holsteiner Charme umgibt den Ort und das Haus.

Das Bauwerk ist eingeschossig, mit einem Dachgeschoss. Die Baumassen sind durch einen Hauswirtschaftsraum verbunden. Zwei Wohnungen von 120 m² und 75 m² finden Platz in der Holzkonstruktion. Die Terrassen und Wohnräume sind nach Süden und Westen ausgerichtet, so dass die Sonne, sobald sie scheint, das Haus wirksam besonnt.

Besonders charmant ist die Verbindung von Moderne und den schönen, einfachen Details. Das Maritime und Nordische wurde hier in liebevoller Gestaltung in Form von Pergolen, Lattenbrüstungen und Sprossenfenstern aufgenommen. Innen verbreiten warme Holzfussböden, weiße Wände und moderne Bäder und Küchen eine angemessene Urlaubsatmosphäre.

Auf der Gartenseite lassen sich alle Fenstertüren bis zum Boden öffnen und sorgen so für eine Verbindung von Garten und Wohnräumen. Eine umlaufende Holzterrasse bietet Platz für Sonnenstühle, Tische und dient als Umlaufbahn für Kinderfahrräder.

Two brilliant white buildings stand on the beach of St. Peter-Ording with views of the North Sea. In warm weather the holiday attributes and atmosphere of this Nordic maritime location are comparable with the Mediterranean. The peninsular around St. Peter-Ording offers excellent possibilities for beach and sea holidays. Broad beaches, green meadows and hidden coves form the backdrop to the elegant construction of the Böhl beach house. The plot of more than 900m² lies directly behind a natural dune and forms part of a holiday home site. The location and the house exude Schleswig-Holstein charm.
The building has one floor and an attic. A utility room connects the sections of the building. Two apartments of 120m² and 75m² are housed within the wooden construction. The terraces and living spaces face south and west, so that the house is bathed in sunlight from early in the morning.

Particularly charming is the combination of modern elements and beautiful, simple details. Maritime and Nordic themes are reflected in the thoughtful design in the form of pergolas, slatted railings and transom windows. In the interior warm wooden floorboards, white walls and modern bathrooms and kitchens exude the requisite holiday atmosphere. On the garden side all the French doors can be fully opened, thereby merging the garden and the living spaces. A circulating wooden terrace offers space for sun loungers, tables and for children to ride bicycles.

Strandhäuser

Deutschland | Germany   Sellin   Insel Rügen, Ostsee | Island Rügen, Baltic Sea

Weißer Steg 8, D-18586 Sellin
www.strandhaeuser-sellin.de, info@die-strandhaeuser.de
Tel.+ 49 38303 85 222

Fertigstellung | date of completion: 2010
Architekt | architect: Wolfgang Warnkross, D-Stralsund
Architektur | architecture: modern
Typ | accommodation: Ferienhäuser | holiday houses
Einheiten|units: 9 Häuser | houses

Sellin gehört neben Binz und Göhren auf Rügen zu den beliebtesten Urlaubsorten auf der Insel. Bekannt ist Sellin durch die alte kaiserzeitliche Flaniermeile Wilhelmstraße. Diese geht in Richtung Meer in die Seebrücke über. Sie ist 394 Meter lang und zieht durch das Brückenhaus hunderte von Touristen an. Besonders magisch wirkt die Seebrücke, wenn die Sonne untergeht. Dann wird sie in ein Meer von Lichterpunkten getaucht.
Von Sellin aus ist das nahe liegende Mönchgut mit seinen sanften Hügeln und weiten Stränden in nur drei Kilometern erreichbar. Freizeitangebote liegen auch nur 100 Meter von den neuen Strandhäusern entfernt: Der Strand selber.

Die Strandhäuser sind konsequent modern geplant worden. Die weißen, kubischen Bauten reflektieren die Strandlage durch den strahlendhellen Putz und die eleganten, schwarzen Fensterrahmen. Holzterrassen bieten bei gutem Wetter einen Freiluftaufenthalt. Die Bauten haben Namen wie Feuerstein, Meereslust oder Wolkenlos. Die Größen der Bauten variieren von 90 bis 110 m² Wohnfläche, jeweils über zwei Etagen verteilt.
Die Einrichtung ist klar, modern und nordisch. Viele Farbpunkte setzen Akzente in den ansonsten warmen Grundtönen. Alle Bäder sind modern und mit den neuesten Details eingerichtet.

Die Planung der 2010 fertig gestellten Anlage mit den insgesamt neun Häusern stammt von dem Architekten Wolfgang Warnkross aus Stralsund.

Along with Binz and Göhren on the island of Rügen, Sellin is amongst the most popular holiday resorts on the island. Sellin is renowned for its old imperial elegant strolling promenade of Wilhelm Street. In the direction of the sea this leads onto the Seebrücke bridge. It is 394 metres long and attracts hundreds of tourists with its bridge house. The Seebrücke is particularly magical when the sun is setting. Then it glitters in a sea of sparkling light. From Sellin it is only three kilometres to the nearby Mönch estate with gently rolling hills and extensive beaches. Leisure possibilities are only 100 metres away from the new beach houses: the beach itself.

The beach houses were planned in a consistently modern style. The white cubed buildings reflect the beach location with their shiny white plaster and the elegant black window frames. In good weather wooden terraces provide open air space. The buildings have names like Feuerstein (Flintstone), Meereslust (Sea Delight) or Wolkenlos (Cloudless). The size of the buildings varies with a living space of 90m² to 110m², divided between two floors. The interior is simple, modern and Nordic. Many patches of colour add accents to the otherwise warm basic tones. All the bathrooms are modern and equipped with the newest details.

The planning of the site completed in 2010 with the total of nine houses was undertaken by the architect Wolfgang Warnkross from Stralsund.

The Balancing Barn

Großbritannien | Great Britain   Thorington   Grafschaft Suffolk | Suffolk

Thornington Rd, UK-IP19 9JG Thorington
www.living-architecture.co.uk, admin@living-architecture.co.uk

Fertigstellung | date of completion: 2010
Architekt | architect: MVRDV, NL-Rotterdam, Jurgen Bey, NL-Rotterdam
Architektur | architecture: modern
Typ | accommodation: Ferienhaus | holiday house
Einheiten | units: 1 Haus | 1 Haus

Nähert man sich dem Gebäude entlang der baumbestandenen Einfahrt, sieht man zuerst ein kleines und in seiner schlichten Form der archetypischen Gestalt einer Scheune gleichendes Gebäude. Erst bei näherer Betrachtung und spätestens beim Umlaufen erkennt man die unglaubliche Weiterführung über das abgestufte Gelände als ein in weiten Teilen freischwebendes Wohnhaus.

Die sogenannte „Balancing Barn" ist Teil des „living architecture" Projektes um Alain de Botton. Living architecture produziert hochwertige Ferienbauten, um moderne Bauten der Allgemeinheit durch Ferienmietungen erfahrbar zu machen.
Das Balancing Barn wurde als Stahlkonstruktion von den niederländischen Architekten MVRDV auf Anfrage von Living Architecture entwickelt und in den letzten Jahren umgesetzt. Der Baugrund selbst liegt inmitten des Naturreservates Suffolk und gehörte früher dem Suffolk Wildlife Trust. Dieser schützt aktiv die umliegende Fauna und Flora, was dem Vorhaben neben seiner architektonischen Herausforderung auch einen engagierten und nachhaltigen Umgang mit der Natur auferlegte.
Das Gebäude selbst ist in seiner Ausrichtung ganz auf die Wahrnehmung des Außenraumes durch seine Bewohner ausgelegt. Das Raumprogramm orientiert

sich an dem eines großzügigen Ferienhauses mit einer Reihe von Zimmern mit en suite Bädern, Küche und Essbereich. Spektakulär aber ist besonders der große Aufenthaltsraum am Ende der 15 Meter langen Auskragung und seinem fantastischem Panoramablick über die umliegenden Hügel. Durch Glasflächen in Dach-und Bodenbereich wird der Ausblick noch zusätzlich verstärkt.

Die Innenarchitektur wurde sorgfältig vom Studio Makkink & Bey gestaltet und kann als eine erfolgreiche Fusion klassischer englischer und holländischer Moderne verstanden werden.
Eine schmale und etwas versteckte Treppe führt vom Wohnbereich hinaus auf die tieferliegende Ebene des weitläufigen Gartens. Von hieraus kann man das prachtvolle Wechselspiel der hochreflektierenden Edelstahlaußenhülle mit den seitlich gepflanzten Bäumen und dem Tageslicht wahrnehmen.

Eine Schwingschaukel am Ende der Auskragung rundet das Erlebnis spielerisch ab und versinnbildlicht praktisch den Namen des Hauses.

Approaching the building along the tree-lined driveway, at first you see a small building whose simple form is that of an archetypal barn. Only on closer observation can one appreciate the extraordinary extension across the terraced site as a largely freely floating residential house. The so-called 'Balancing Barn' is part of the 'Living Architecture' project, founded by Alain de Botton. Living Architecture creates high-end holiday residences which offer the general public the experience of contemporary architecture through holiday rentals.

The Balancing Barn was developed and realised as a steel construction by the Dutch architects MVRDV, commissioned by Living Architecture and opened to the public in October 2010. The building is situated in the heart of a Suffolk nature reserve, formerly part of the Suffolk Wildlife Trust, which actively protects the surrounding flora and fauna. So apart from the architectural challenge, the project also demanded a committed and sustainable treatment of nature. The building is oriented to give occupants maximum appreciation of the natural surroundings.

The accommodation is modelled on that of a generous holiday home, with a series of rooms all with en suite bathrooms and a substantial kitchen and dining area. The large communal room at the end of the 15-metre-long protruding building is especially spectacular, with its fantastic panoramic view over the surrounding hills. The views are highlighted further by the glass surfaces in the roof and floor.

The interior design was carefully created by Studio Makkink & Bey to create a successful fusion of the classical English and Dutch modern eras. Narrow and partially hidden stairs lead out of the living space into the lower-lying spacious garden. From here one can appreciate the magnificent interplay of the highly reflecting stainless steel exterior with the adjacent trees and daylight.

A swing at the end of the protruding building completes the experience with a playful twist and symbolises the name of the farm in practical terms.

The Dune House

Großbritannien | Great Britain   Thorpeness   Grafschaft Suffolk, Nordsee | Suffolk, North Sea

Aldeburgh Rd, UK-IP16 4NR Thorpeness
www.living-architecture.co.uk, admin@living-architecture.co.uk

Fertigstellung | date of completion: 2010
Architekt | architect: JVA Jarmund/Vigsnæs Architects NO-Oslo
                                    with Mole Architects
Architektur | architecture: modern
Typ | accommodation: Ferienhaus| holiday house
Einheiten | units: 1 Haus | 1 house

Nordöstlich von London liegt an der Kanalküste in dem kleinen Städtchen Thorpeness ein neues Strandhaus das eine besondere Architektur auszeichnet. Das norwegische Architekturbüro Jarmund Vigsnaes Architects wurden von „living architecture" (siehe auch Balancing Barn und Shingle House) gebeten, ein passendes, neuartiges Strandhaus zu konzipieren.

Da die Architekten über eine große Erfahrung in der Planung von besonderen Häusern haben, konnte nichts weniger als ein herausragendes Bauwerk erwartet werden. Und dieses haben sie abgeliefert. Das Haus ist ultramodern und traditionell in einer Form. Alle Attribute frühmodernen Bauens sind berücksichtigt: Sockelbildung, Auflösung des unteren Geschosses, freie Formfindung. Als Gegengestaltung dazu wurde das Dach an traditionelle Formen angelehnt. Auch die dunkle Farbe spiegelt eher die lokalen Bauten wieder. In Kürze: Ein Haus in dem sich alle Generationen und alle Interessen wieder finden können.
In dem Haus können bis zu neun Personen ihren Urlaub verbringen.

Im Inneren herrschen gedämpfte Töne und eine kultivierte Moderne. Das Erdgeschoss wirkt durch die komplette Verglasung um das Haus herum leicht und aufgeräumt. Hier befinden sich Küche, Wohnraum mit einem Kamin. Die Aussicht ist spektakulär, behindern ja kaum tragende Bauteile die Sicht.
In den Obergeschossen befinden sich die Schlafräume. Diese sind durch die komplexe Geometrie des Daches verwinkelt und aufregend gestaltet. Überraschende Aussichten und Blickwinkel bilden ein wunderbares Labyrinth auf kleinem Raum. Hier herrscht Kieferholz vor und vermittelt so das Dachraumgefühl.

Der Aussenbereich ist durch die Absenkung des Hauses in das Terrain definiert. Dieser clevere Trick birgt etwas geborgenes, was gegen die moderne Glasfront des Erdgeschosses wirkt. Vielleicht kann man hier die Assoziation zu einer Sandburg sehen. Die Gegend ist geprägt durch die vielen Windmühlen. Eine Eigenart sind die über 300 kleinen Strandhäuser, die bunt gemischt als kleine Abstell- und Umkleideorte dienen. Vielleicht standen beide beschriebenen Typologien als Pate für das Design des Dune House.

To the north-east of London on the Channel coast in the small town of Thorpeness lies a new beach house with special architectural features. The Norwegian architecture bureau Jarmund Vigsnaes Architects were commissioned by 'Living Architecture' (see also Balancing Barn and Shingle House) to design a suitably innovative beach house. As the architects have a wealth of experience in planning special houses, nothing less than an outstanding building was to be expected and was indeed delivered.
The house is ultra-modern and also in some ways traditional. All the features of early modern building have been taken into account: the creation of the base, the composition of the ground floor, the free determination of form. In contrast the roof adopts traditional forms. The dark colour scheme also reflects the local buildings. Basically it is a house where all generations can feel at home and all interests can be catered for.

The house provides holiday accommodation for up to nine people.
The interior is dominated by subdued colour tones and cultivated modernity. The ground floor appears light and neat with its complete glazing encircling the house. Here one can find the kitchen and living room with a fireplace. The view is spectacular, uninterrupted by supporting building elements.
On the upper floors are the bedrooms. These have a winding and exciting design owing to the complex geometry of the roof. Surprising views and perspectives create a wonderful labyrinth within a small space. Pine wood is dominant, conveying the feeling of an attic to the occupant.

The outdoor space is defined by the embedding of the house into the terrain. This clever trick creates the impression of being snug and hidden away in the dunes, in contrast to the modern glass front of the ground floor.
Perhaps one can see the similarity to a sandcastle. The area is characterised by many windmills. A further peculiarity are the more than 300 small beach huts, a colourful collection that serves as storage spaces and changing rooms. Perhaps both of these typologies were an inspiration for the design of Dune House.

The Shingle House

Großbritannien | Great Britain   Dungeness   Grafschaft Kent, Nordsee | Kent, North Sea

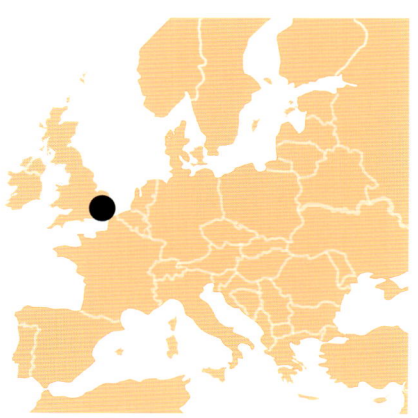

Dugnesess Rd, UK-TN29 9NE Dungeness
www.living-architecture.co.uk, admin@living-architecture.co.uk

Fertigstellung | date of completion: 2010
Architekt | architect: NORD Architecture, UK-Glasgow
Architektur | architecture: modern
Typ | accommodation: Ferienhaus | holiday house
Einheiten | units: 1 Haus | 1 house

An einem der wohl poetischsten und zugleich un-typischsten Orte Englands befindet sich in der unter Naturschutz gestellten Bucht des Shingle Beach of Dungeness das ebenso untypische Shingle House. Stark geprägt von der schlichten und wildroman-tischen Geographie von Dungeness entwickelten das Team von Nord Architecture das Gebäude für „living architecture" (siehe auch Balancing Barn und Dune House) aus mehreren unterschiedlich großen Teilen, die jeweils in einer schlichten, fast rudimentären Form gehalten sind.

Angelehnt an die hier üblichen Fischerhütten sind sie außen mit Holzlatten verschalt und ganz in Schwarz gehalten. Dies verleiht dem Ganzen eine leicht entrückte Eleganz und dominiert leicht monu-mental die Umgebung.

Drehbare Holzblenden, großzügige Öffnungen und schmale Fensterschlitze geben je nach Bedarf den Blick frei auf diese einzigartige Landschaft.

Das Hauptgebäude besitzt drei Doppelzimmer mit Wohnraum und offenem Kamin im Erdgeschoss sowie einem weiteren Zimmer im Obergeschoss. Daran angeschlossen befindet sich das Badehaus mit einer schwarzpolierten Betonwanne, die einen direkten Ausblick auf die Landschaft erlaubt. Vervollständigt wird der Komplex vom Essbereich mit Küche, die auf den dazwischenliegenden Patio geöffnet werden können.

Das Interieur ist ähnlich schlicht gestaltet wie das Äußere und wird dominiert von hellen Sichtbeton-elementen, wie dem Kamin oder der Küchenzeile. lle Wände sind mit Holzlatten verblendet, die in Weiß gehalten sind. Der leicht violettfarbene, dunkle Holzboden ist inspiriert von den sommerlichen purpurnen Blütenteppichen der Strandvegetation.

In der Umgebung des Shingle House finden sich der alte Leuchtturm in Dungeness und das historische Örtchen Rye mit dem Rye Castle und dem Wohn-haus des Literaten Henry James.

In what is undoubtedly one of the most poetic and also most unusual places in England lies the equally unusual Shingle House, on the shingle beach at Dungeness, which has been placed under nature protection.

Strongly influenced by the stark and wildly romantic geography of Dungeness, the team from Nord Architecture developed the building for 'Living Architecture' (see also The Balancing Barn and The Dune House) as a cluster of simple, almost rudimentary buildings.

The black, wooden, slatted exterior cladding is reminiscent of the fishing huts typical of the area. This lends the whole a somewhat other-worldly elegance and monumentality, giving it presence in the landscape.

Pivotable wooden shutters, generous openings and narrow window slits afford open views over this unique landscape.

The main building comprises three double rooms with a living room and open fireplace on the ground floor and a further room on the upper floor. The adjacent bathing space has a black polished concrete bathtub with direct views out to the surroundings. The complex is completed with a dining area and kitchen, which open out onto the patio in between.

The interior has a simple design similar to that of the exterior and is dominated by light decorative concrete elements, like the fireplace or the kitchen unit. All walls are veneered with white wooden panels. The violet-tinted dark floor is inspired by the purple flowers which carpet the beach in summer.

In the vicinity of Shingle House are the old lighthouse in Dungeness and the historical little town of Rye with Rye Castle and the house of the literary man Henry James.

Treehotel

Schweden | Sweden   Harads   Nordschweden | North Sweden

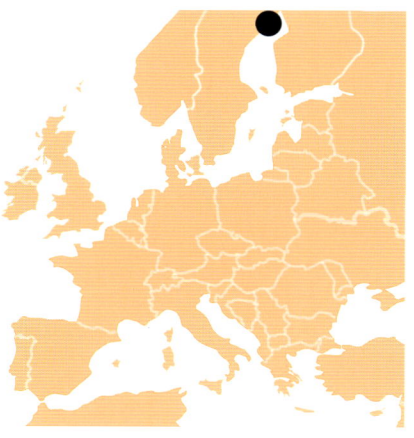

Edeforsväg 2a, SE-96024 Harads
www.treehotel.se, info@treehotel.se
Tel. + 46 928 104 03

Fertigstellung | date of completion: 2010
Architekt | architect: siehe Text | see text
Architektur | architecture: modern
Typ | accommodation: Hotel
Einheiten | units: 6 Baumhäuser | 6 treehouses

Die Vulkaninsel Stromboli ist von jeher bekannt als Rückzugs- und Inspirationsort für Schriftsteller, Künstler und Menschen, die das einfache maritime Leben schätzen. Auch Naturliebhaber und Freunde süditalienischer Lebensart kommen an diesem idyllischen Fleck der Erde auf ihre Kosten.

Traumhaft liegt die Villa La Pergola oberhalb einer kleinen, fast privaten Strandbucht und bietet die ideale Kulisse für vollkommene Entspannung.
Vor über 100 Jahren ist oberhalb der kleinen Bucht Piscilla das typisch eolianische Fischerhaus erbaut worden. Zwei geräumige Zimmer und eine kleine Küche sowie eine vorgelagerte und mit Bambusrohr überdachte Terrasse bildeten die einfache Wohneinheit. Wenige Meter weiter stand ein kleines Lagerhaus. Die 60 cm dicken Wände des Hauses wurden aus lokalen Lavasteinen gebaut.

Im Jahr 1998 übernahm der heutige Eigentümer die Villa La Pergola und ein Jahr später erfolgte die Sanierung und Renovierung aller Räume des Hauses. Im Herbst 2009 und im Frühjahr 2010 wurden weitere Ausbauarbeiten im und am gesamten Haus durchgeführt. Dabei wurden auch die Terrassenflächen saniert und erweitert, eine dritte große Zisterne angelegt und ein kleiner Anbau auf dem Gelände realisiert. Damit hat die Villa La Pergola einen Zustand und Standard erreicht, um auch in den nächsten Jahren den Anspruch an einen typisch süditalienischen Urlaub bieten zu können.
Auf 170 m² bietet das Haus Platz für sechs Personen. Der direkte Zugang zur Bucht liefert neben dem fantastischen Blick von der fast 200 m² großen Terrasse eine einzigartige Ferienmöglichkeit. Ein typisches Detail der Bauten auf den eolischen Inseln ist die in das Geländer integrierte Sitzbank. So kann man mit Blick auf das Meer und die Terrasse die Stunden verbringen.

Im Inneren bietet das Haus einen lang gestreckten Grundriss, der eine erfrischende Durchlüftung erlaubt. Die drei Schlafzimmer sind an einem seitlichen Schenkel untergebracht, so dass sie ein L bilden und der Terrasse eine ruhige Privatsphäre bieten.
Das Haus ist mit regional-typischen Einrichtungsgegenständen ausgestattet. Die Materialien entsprechen dem mediterranen Umfeld.

The volcanic island of Stromboli has always been known as a place of retreat and inspiration for authors, artists and people who appreciate simple maritime life. Nature lovers and those in favour of the southern Italian lifestyle also get their money's worth by coming to this idyllic part of the world.

The villa La Pergola lies in a picturesque location above a small, almost private sandy bay and offers the ideal backdrop for complete relaxation.
More than 100 years ago the typical Aeolian fisherman's house was built above the small Piscilla cove. Two spacious rooms, a small kitchen and a terrace roofed with bamboo canes in front of the house formed a simple living unit. A few metres away stood a small storage hut. The 60cm thick walls of the house were built with local lava stones.

In 1998 the current owners took over the villa La Pergola and a year later they upgraded and renovated all the rooms in the house. In autumn 2009 and in spring 2010 further upgrades in and around the whole house were carried out. The terrace surfaces were renovated and extended, a third big cistern was added and a small extension was built on the plot of land. The villa La Pergola thereby achieved a state and standard that would enable it to fulfil the requirements of a typical southern Italian holiday in years to come.
The 170m² house offers accommodation for six people. The direct access to the bay and the fantastic view from the nearly 200m² terrace provide a unique holiday experience. A typical feature of

buildings on the Aeolian islands is the seating bench integrated into balcony railings. In this way one can spend hours enjoying the views of the sea and the terrace.

The interior of the house has an elongated layout, enabling refreshing ventilation. The three bedrooms are housed in an arm to the side, so that they form an L shape and give the terrace quiet privacy.
The house has typical regional furnishings. The materials are in keeping with the Mediterranean surroundings.

Villa Vals

Schweiz | Switzerland   Vals   Graubünden, Valsertal | Grisons, Valservalley

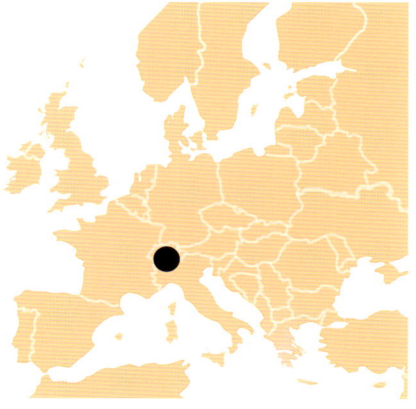

Poststraße 38, Rota Härd, CH-7132 Vals
www.villavals.ch, info@villavals.ch
Tel. +31 20 788 99 00

Fertigstellung | date of completion: 2009
Architekt | architect: Bjarne Mastenbroek (SeARCH), NL-Amsterdam;
                        Christian Müller (CMA), NL-Rotterdam
Architektur | architecture: modern
Typ | accommodation: Ferienhaus | holiday house
Einheiten|units: 1 Haus | 1 house

In nächster Nähe zu den weltbekannten Thermen von Vals (Architekt Peter Zumthor) befindet sich im Kanton Graubünden dieses unkonventionelle Gebäude. Eingegraben in die Erde wollten die Architekten von SeARCH & CMA es bewusst den Blicken der Therme entziehen und gleichzeitig sensibel mit dem lokalen Kontext umgehen. Schon die Eingangssituation zeigt den besonderen Ansatz der Holländischen Architekten in einer für Sie eher untypischen Topografie. So dient eine nebenstehende alte Scheune als eigentlicher Zugang, die über einen Tunnel mit der neugeschaffenen Ferienwohnung verbunden ist. Dies zieht sich auch im Inneren in einer Art „Wohnlandschaft„ weiter fort, wobei die Geschosse ineinander verzahnt sind und höchst unterschiedliche Raumqualitäten durch ein Verspringen der jeweiligen Ebenen entstehen.

Der eigentliche Innenausbau wurde unter Anderem vom Studio JVM entwickelt und wird von einem Wechselspiel klarer Lienen industrieller Werkstoffe wie Sichtbeton und warmen Holzeinbauten dominiert. Die insgesamt 160m² Wohnfläche verteilen sich dabei über insgesamt zwei Geschosse und bieten Platz für ca. 10 Personen.

Eine im hinteren Teil befindliche Treppe verbindet drei Schlafräume inklusive Badezimmern im Obergeschoss mit dem Wohn- und Essbereich sowie einer Bibliothek mit einer weiteren Schlafmöglichkeit im Erdgeschoss. Große Schiebelemente geben dieser Ebene zusätzlich die Möglichkeit diese Funktionsräume je nach Bedarf als Ganzes zu verbinden oder zu separieren. Belichtet wird das Gebäude über einen ca. 60m² großen Patio. Seine in Hangrichtung abfallende Ellipsenform lässt dabei großzügige Fensteröffnungen zu, die faszinierende Blicke auf die den Ort umgebende Bergwelt freigeben.

Die Fassade des Patio ist Naturstein bzw. Sichtbeton gehalten und an seiner niedrigsten Stelle über ein paar Holzstufen an zu den Almwiesen hin erschlossen. Insgesamt handelt es sich um den höchst interessanten Versuch einer Fusion zeitgenössischer Architektur mit den Anforderungen einer gefährdeten Bergwelt. Allein die etwas grobe Absicherung zum Schutz nichts ahnender Wanderer zeugt von der experimentierfreudigen Weiterentwicklung dieses Ansatzes.

This unconventional building is located in the canton of Graubünden in the close proximity of the world-famous thermal spa of Vals by the Swiss architect Peter Zumthor. It is embedded in the ground, as the architects of SeARCH & CMA were consciously seeking to conceal it from view from the spa and to treat the local context sensitively. The entrance is already indicative of the particular approach of the Dutch architects, in this topography that is untypical for them. And so an adjacent old barn serves as the actual entrance, which is connected to the newly built holiday apartment via a tunnel. This continues into the interior with a sort of living landscape, with interlocking storeys whose split levels create very varied spatial qualities.

The actual interior conversion was designed amongst others by Studio JVM and is dominated by the juxta-position of clear lines of industrial materials such as decorative concrete with warm wooden fixtures. The living space totalling 160m² is spread over two floors and can accommodate about 10 people.
A staircase at the rear connects three bedrooms comprising bathrooms on the top floor with a living and dining area, as well as a library offering additional accommodation on the ground floor.

Large sliding elements provide the further option as required to combine these rooms into one large space or to separate them. The building is lightened up by a 60m² patio. Its downwardly sloped elliptical form allows generous window openings, which afford fascinating views of the surrounding alpine world.

The patio façade is natural stone and decorative con-crete and at its lowest point is connected to alpine meadows via a couple of wooden steps. Overall it represents a highly interesting attempt to fuse contemporary architecture with the requirements of an endangered mountain environment. Even the rather crude protection for the safety of unsuspecting mountain hikers shows the experimental further development of this approach.

Viura

Spanien | Spain   Álava   Rioja, Baskenland | Rioja, Basque Province

Calle Mayor s/n, Villabuena de Áalva, ES-01307 Álava
www.hotelviura.com, info@hotelviura.com
Tel. +34 945 60 90 00, Fax +34 943 60 94 47

Fertigstellung | date of completion: 2010
Architekt | architect: Designhouses, Spain
Architektur | architecture: modern
Typ | accommodation: Hotel
Einheiten | units: 33 Zimmer | rooms (14 Standard, 15 Luxus, 4 Suiten)

Im Herzen der spanischen Weinregion Rioja kommt man in der urigen Altstadt von Villabuena de Alva an dem im Frühling 2010 eröffneten Hotel Viura kaum vorbei. In unmittelbarer Nachbarschaft zur mittelalterlichen Stadtkirche San Andrés steht es in einem spannungsreichen Kontrast mit dem eher schlichten Kontext der unmittelbaren Umgebung. Dieser Umstand steigert die Wirkung fast noch und führt zu einem architektonischen Feuerwerk an Materialien, Formen und Details. Von außen betrachtet werden formal unterschiedliche „Kisten" gestapelt, die verdreht und gestaffelt dem Baukörper durch eine gezielte Auflösung die Massigkeit nehmen. Beruhigung erfährt der Komplex durch ein ausgewogenes Verhältnis von transparenten Glasflächen und opaken Außenwänden der einzelnen Boxen, die mal in rostigen Stahlplatten, mal in grauem Sichtbeton gehalten sind. Aufgelockert wird die Fassade zudem durch unterschiedlich dimensionierte private Dachterrassen mit deren Begrünung und einem interessanten Spiel von Licht und Schatten der einzelnen Volumen. Überhaupt wurde bei diesem Gebäude dem Ausblick auf die umliegenden Hügel und Bergketten viel Bedeutung geschenkt.

Dem mit solchen Projekten erfahrenem Team von Designhouses lag aber auch viel an einer zeitgenössischen Lösung im Inneren. Auch hier der Versuch modernen Flair mit Elementen baskischer Tradition zu verknüpfen. Besonders das Restaurant im Erdgeschoss profitiert davon und überzeugt mit seinen kühl-eleganten Sichtbetonwänden und den Weinfässern, die sich dekorativ vom schwarzen Hintergrund der Decke abheben. Der Bezug ist bewusst gewählt, ist das Hotel auch Ausgangsort für Erkundungen dieser international bekannten Weinregion.

33 Zimmer und Suiten stehen dem Gast zur Wahl, die alle über separate Bäder und teilweise Privatbalkone verfügen. Das Interieur ist wie die Architektur konsequent modern und technisch zeitgemäß ausgestattet. Und natürlich finden sich in der Zimmerbar einige gute Tropfen der Region, um sich in Ruhe auf den Urlaub einzustimmen.

At the heart of the Spanish wine region Rioja in the quaint old town of Villabuena de Alava one can not miss Hotel Viura, opened in spring 2010. It is in close proximity of the medieval municipal church of San Andrés and stands in marked contrast to the rather simple context of the immediate surroundings. This enhances its impact and creates an architectural fireworks of materials, forms and details. Viewed from the exterior it has the appearance of formally stacked 'boxes' of varying sizes, which are aligned and tiered in a constellation designed to reduce the building's bulkiness. The complex is lent a calm appearance by the balanced interplay of transparent glass surfaces and the opaque exterior walls of the individual boxes, which are encased in rusty steel panels or grey decorative concrete. The façade is lightened up with private roof terraces in varying dimensions, with their greenery and an interesting juxtaposition of light and shade on the different spaces. A lot of emphasis was placed on the views towards the surrounding hills and mountain ranges.

It was also a prime concern of the team from Designhouses who are experienced in such projects to create a contemporary solution for the interior, where they set out to combine modern flair with traditional Basque elements. Especially the ground floor restaurant benefits from that and is impressive with its cool elegant decorative concrete walls and the wine barrels standing out decoratively from the black background of the ceiling. This reference is a conscious choice, as the hotel is also a starting point for tours of this internationally renowned wine region.

More than 30 rooms and suites are available for guests (33 rooms: 14 Viura (standard), 15 Deluxe and 4 suites), all of which have their own bathrooms and in some cases private balconies. The interior furnishings, like the architecture, are consistently and contemporarily modern and technical. And naturally the mini-bar provides some of the region's excellent wines to get oneself in the holiday mood in the comfort of one's own room.

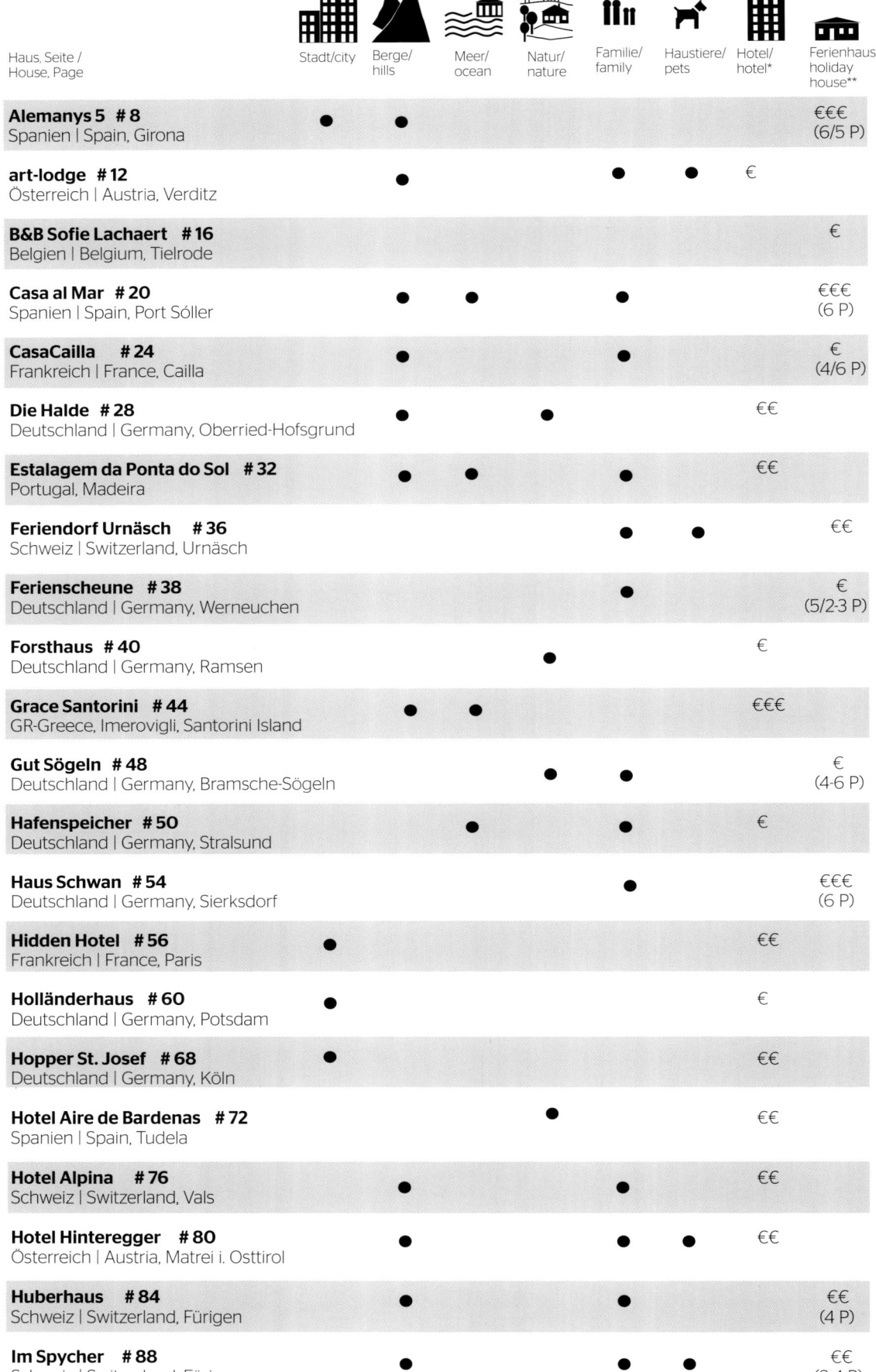

Haus, Seite / House, Page	Stadt/city	Berge/hills	Meer/ocean	Natur/nature	Familie/family	Haustiere/pets	Hotel/hotel*	Ferienhaus/holiday house**
Alemanys 5 #8 Spanien | Spain, Girona	●	●						€€€ (6/5 P)
art-lodge #12 Österreich | Austria, Verditz		●			●	●	€	
B&B Sofie Lachaert #16 Belgien | Belgium, Tielrode							€	
Casa al Mar #20 Spanien | Spain, Port Sóller		●	●		●			€€€ (6 P)
CasaCailla #24 Frankreich | France, Cailla		●			●			€ (4/6 P)
Die Halde #28 Deutschland | Germany, Oberried-Hofsgrund		●		●			€€	
Estalagem da Ponta do Sol #32 Portugal, Madeira		●	●		●		€€	
Feriendorf Urnäsch #36 Schweiz | Switzerland, Urnäsch					●	●		€€
Ferienscheune #38 Deutschland | Germany, Werneuchen					●			€ (5/2-3 P)
Forsthaus #40 Deutschland | Germany, Ramsen				●			€	
Grace Santorini #44 GR-Greece, Imerovigli, Santorini Island		●	●				€€€	
Gut Sögeln #48 Deutschland | Germany, Bramsche-Sögeln				●	●			€ (4-6 P)
Hafenspeicher #50 Deutschland | Germany, Stralsund			●		●		€	
Haus Schwan #54 Deutschland | Germany, Sierksdorf					●			€€€ (6 P)
Hidden Hotel #56 Frankreich | France, Paris	●						€€	
Holländerhaus #60 Deutschland | Germany, Potsdam	●						€	
Hopper St. Josef #68 Deutschland | Germany, Köln	●						€€	
Hotel Aire de Bardenas #72 Spanien | Spain, Tudela				●			€€	
Hotel Alpina #76 Schweiz | Switzerland, Vals		●			●		€€	
Hotel Hinteregger #80 Österreich | Austria, Matrei i. Osttirol		●			●	●	€€	
Huberhaus #84 Schweiz | Switzerland, Fürigen		●			●			€€ (4 P)
Im Spycher #88 Schweiz | Switzerland, Fürigen		●			●	●		€€ (2-4 P)
Indulgence Divine #92 Malta, Birgu	●		●				€€	

*/** Legende siehe # 179 | legend see # 179

Haus, Seite / House, Page	Stadt/city	Berge/ hills	Meer/ ocean	Natur/ nature	Familie/ family	Haustiere/ pets	Hotel/ hotel*	Ferienhaus/ holiday house**
Insular Apartments #96 Deutschland	Germany, Norderney			●		●			€€/€€€ (2/4/6 P)
Kavaliershaus #98 Deutschland	Germany,, Fincken				●		●	€	
La Maison d'Ulysse #102 Frankreich	France, Ulysse				●	●		€€	
La Romana #106 Spanien	Spain, La Romana				●			€€	
Les Cols Pavellons #108 Spanien	Spain, Olot			●				€€€	
Haus Liebing #110 Deutschland	Germany, Dresden	●							€€
Manzara #114 Türkei	Turkey, Istanbul	●		●				€€	
Nebesa #118 Slowenien	Slovenia, Kobarid		●						€€€ (2 P)
Nordic Watercolour #122 Schweden	Sweden, Shärhamn			●				€€	
Refugio Son Pons #124 Spanien	Spain, Campanet-Ullaró			●	●			€€€	
Salvinia Lodge #128 Polen	Poland, Stegna			●		●	●		€ - €€
Spielberg5 #134 Deutschland	Germany, Freiburg	●				●			€€ (8 P)
Skinidin - Black Shed #138 Großbritannien	Great Britain, Skindin	●		●	●	●			€ (2 P)
Strandhaus Böhl #141 Deutschland	Germany, St. Peter Ording			●		●			€€ (8/4 P)
Strandhäuser #146 Deutschland	Germany, Rügen			●		●			€€ (6/8 P)
The Balancing Barn #150 Großbritannien	Great Britain, Thorington					●			€€€ (8 P)
The Dune House #154 Großbritannien	Great Britain, Thorington			●		●	●		€€€ (9 P)
The Shingle House #.158 Großbritannien	Great Britain, Dungeness			●		●	●		€€€ (8 P)
Treehotel #162 Schweden	Sweden, Harads				●			€€€	
Villa La Pergola #166 Italien	Italy, Stromboli			●		●			€€ (2 P)
Villa Vals #170 Schweiz	Switzerland, Vals		●						€€€ (10-12 P)
Viura #174 Spanien	Spain, Alava	●						€€	

* Preise Hotels für ein Standard Doppelzimmer (pro Nacht in der Saison) | prices hotels for a standard double (night/season) :
€ <100 EUR | €€ 100-175 EUR | €€€ > 175 EUR
** Preis Ferienhäuser/Apartments (pro Woche in der Saison) | prices holiday houses & apartments (week/season):
€ <700 EUR €€ | 700-1500 EUR | €€€ >1500 EUR

Abbildungsverzeichnis | list of figures

Titelseite | cover : The Dune House
Rückseite | back side: Alemanys 5

Bildnachweis | photo credits:
Titelbild | cover: The Dune House, Foto | photo: Ivar Kvall

IMPRESSUM

Herausgeber:

 **URLAUBS**ARCHITEKTUR
HOLIDAYARCHITECTURE
www.urlaubsarchitektur.de | www.holidayarchitecture.com
Bozener Straße 6
D-30519 Hannover

Verlag:
archimappublishers
Kaiser Peters Wormuth GbR
Weimarer Str. 32
D-10625 Berlin

Beratung: Hermann Hülsenberg Studio
Texte: Jan Hamer und Nadine Weiland
Lektorat: Martina Wisser
Übersetzung: Lynne Kolar-Thompson
Redaktion und Projektleitung: Jan Hamer und Nils Peters

Bibliografische Information der Deutschen Bibliothek - Die Deutsche Bibliothek
verzeichnet diese Publikation in der Deutschen Nationalbibliografie; detaillierte
bibliografische Daten sind im Internet über http://dhb.ddb.de abrufbar.

Printed in Turkey
ISBN 978-3-940874-11-5
© Copyright 2011
Text und Bild bei den Autoren und dem Verlag
Alle Rechte vorbehalten